Adult Coloring Book
Large Print

50 Cute,Fun, Easy, and Relaxing Coloring Patterns

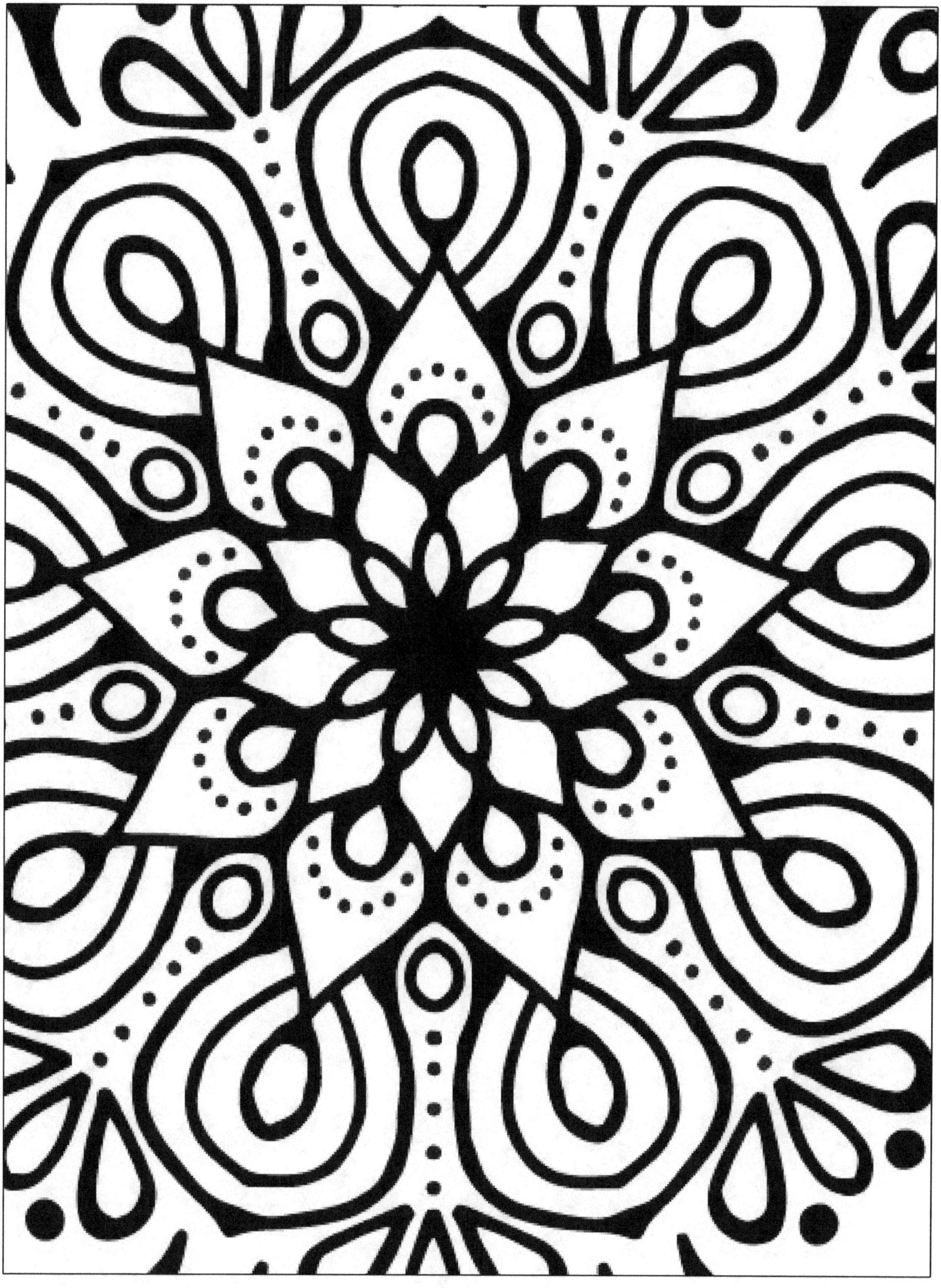

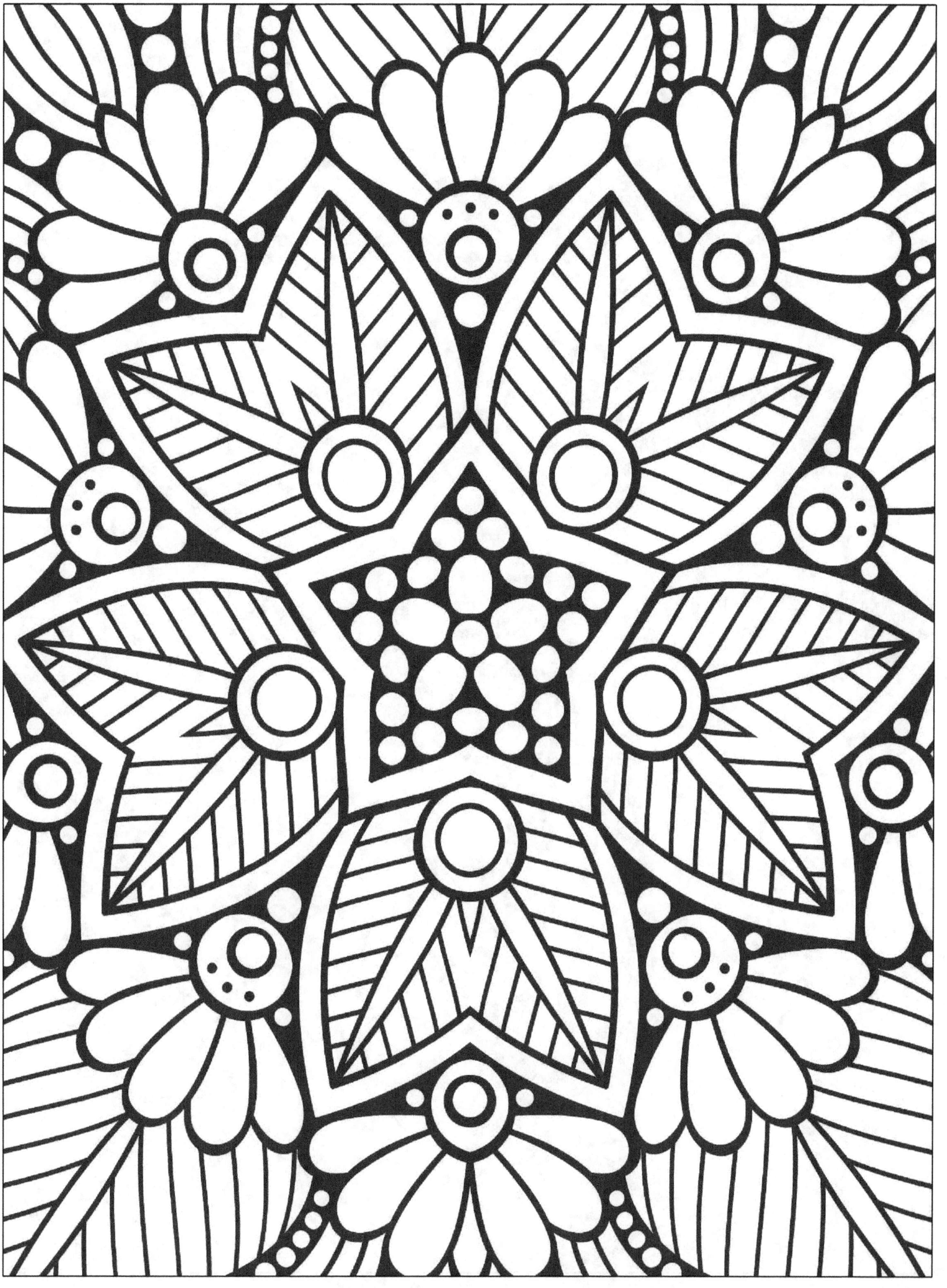

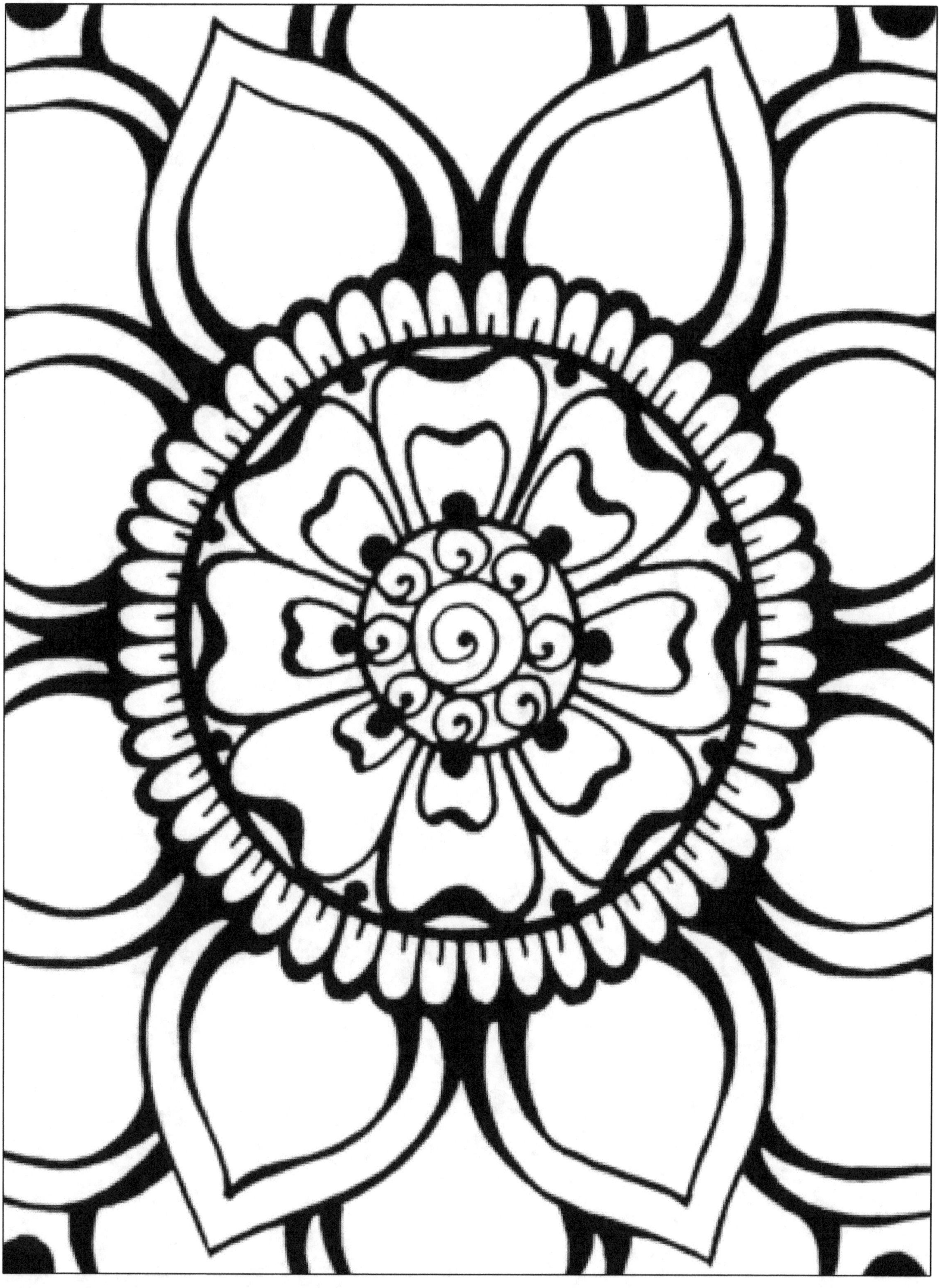

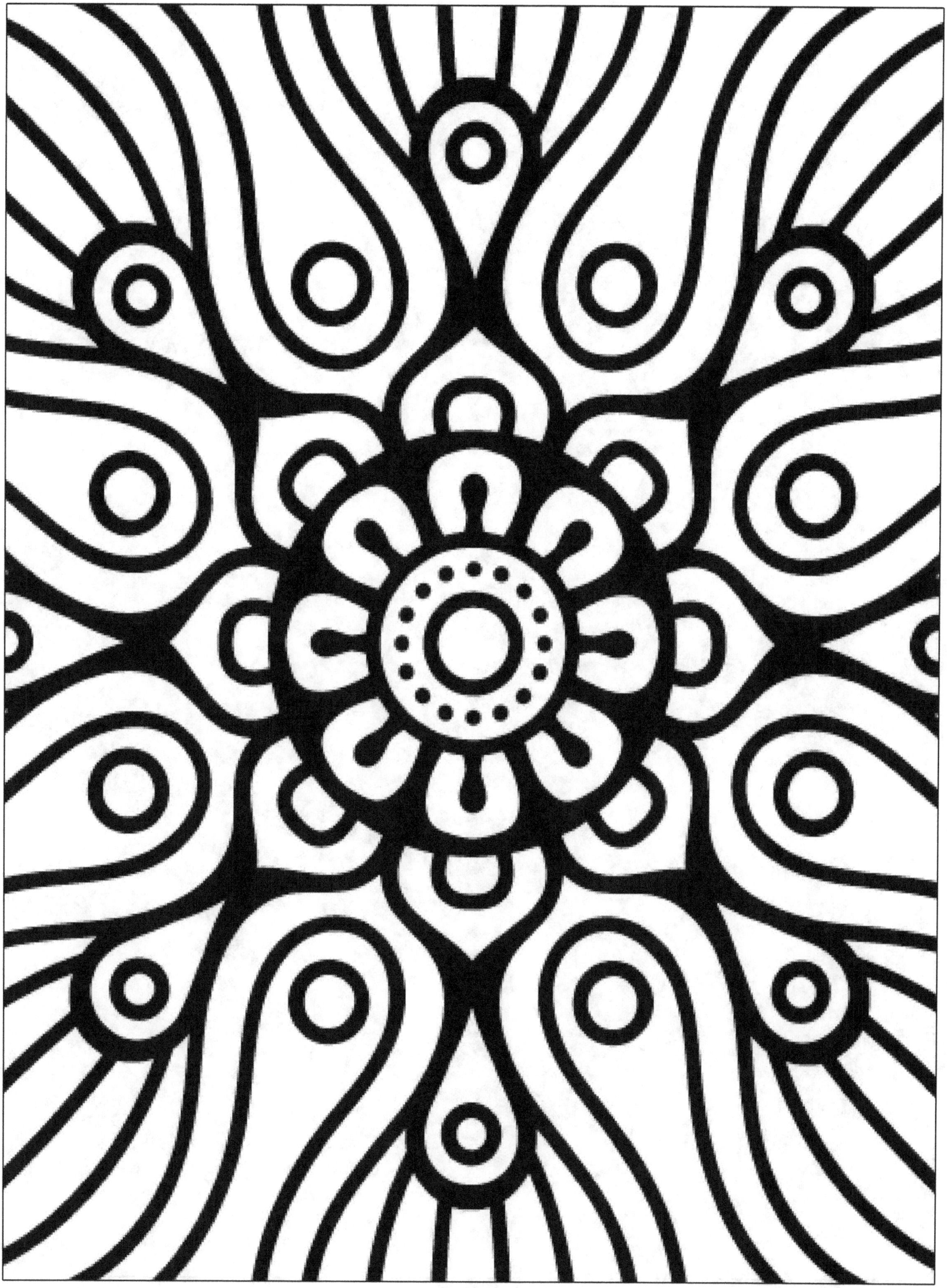

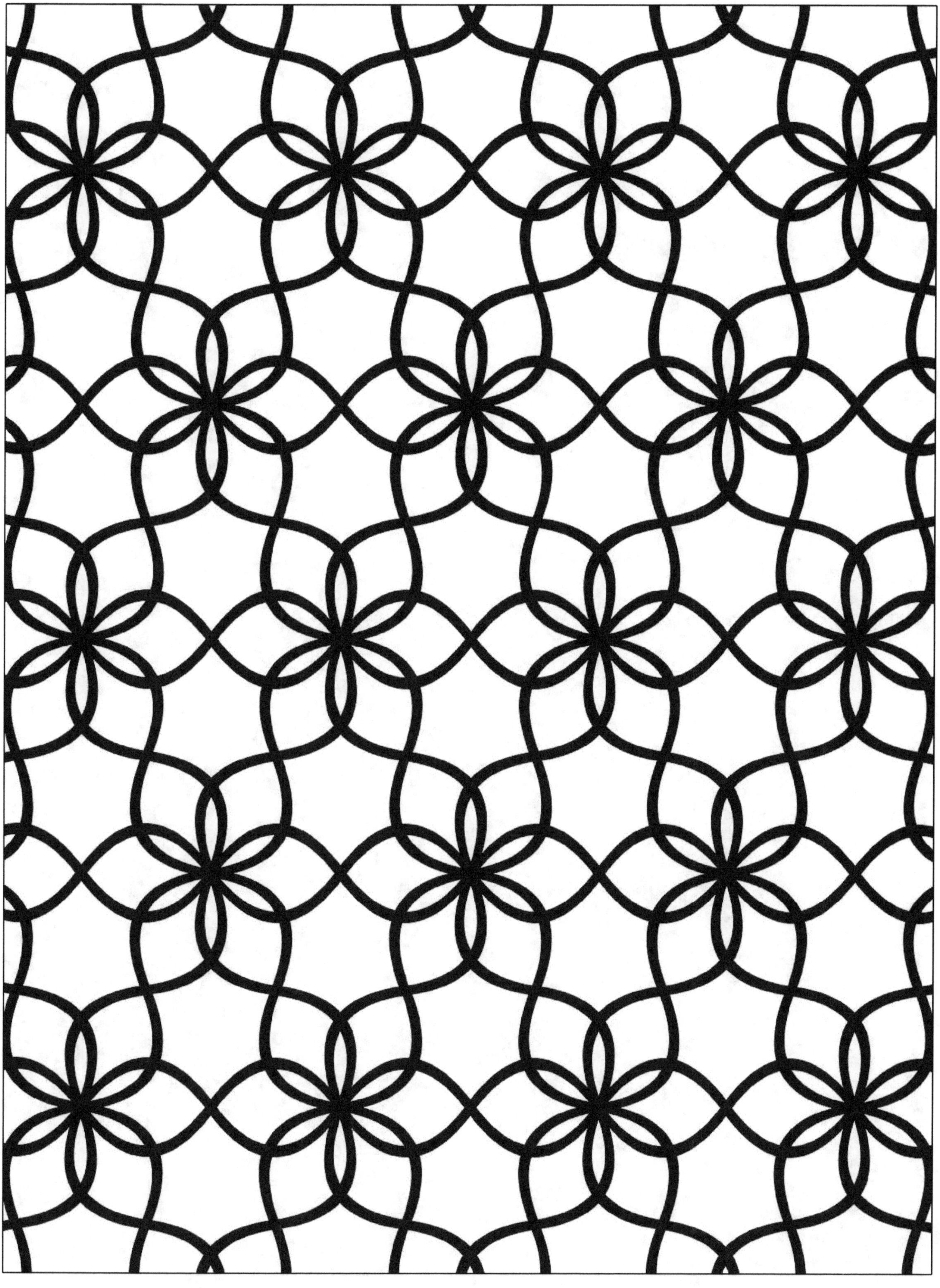

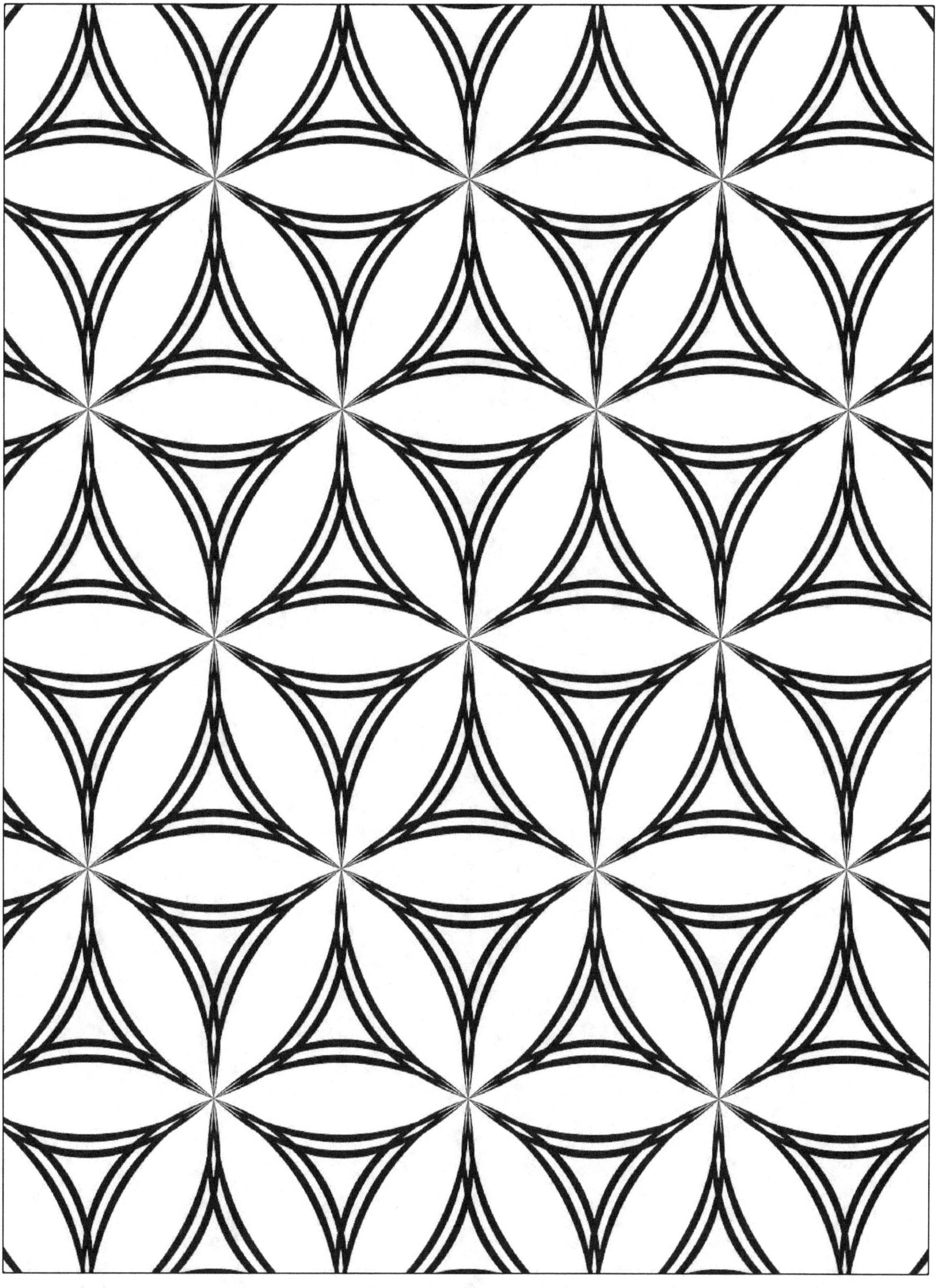

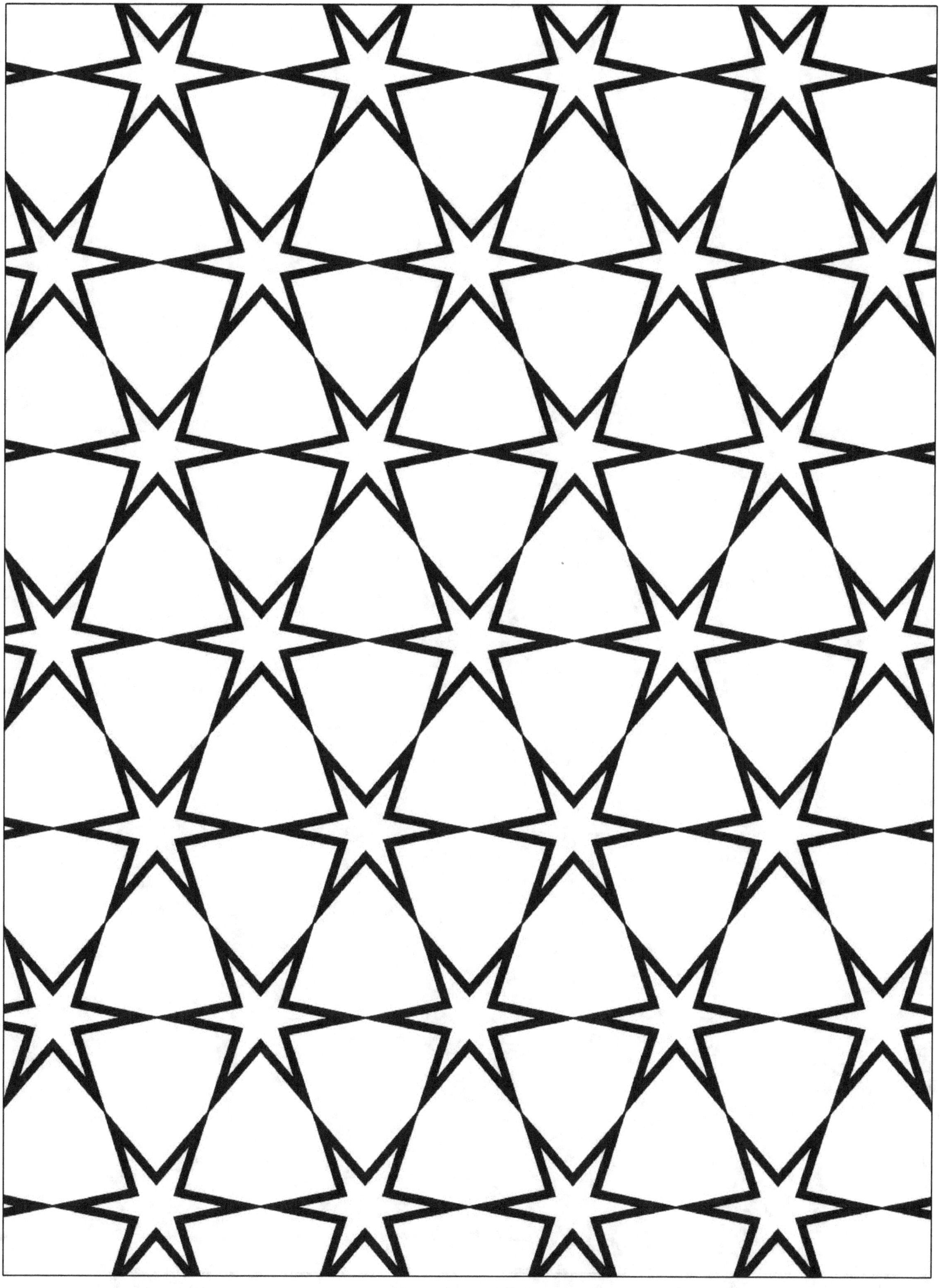

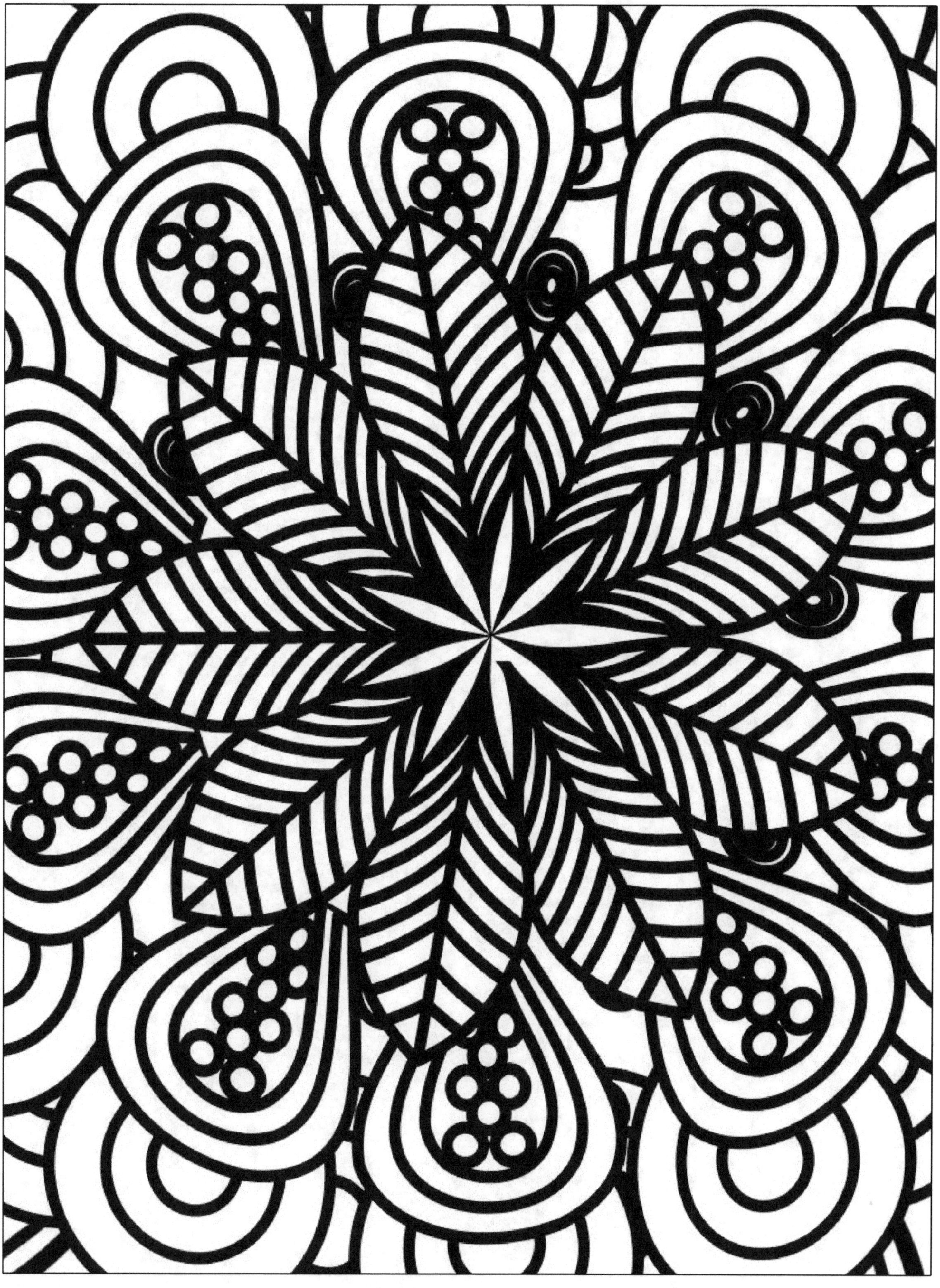

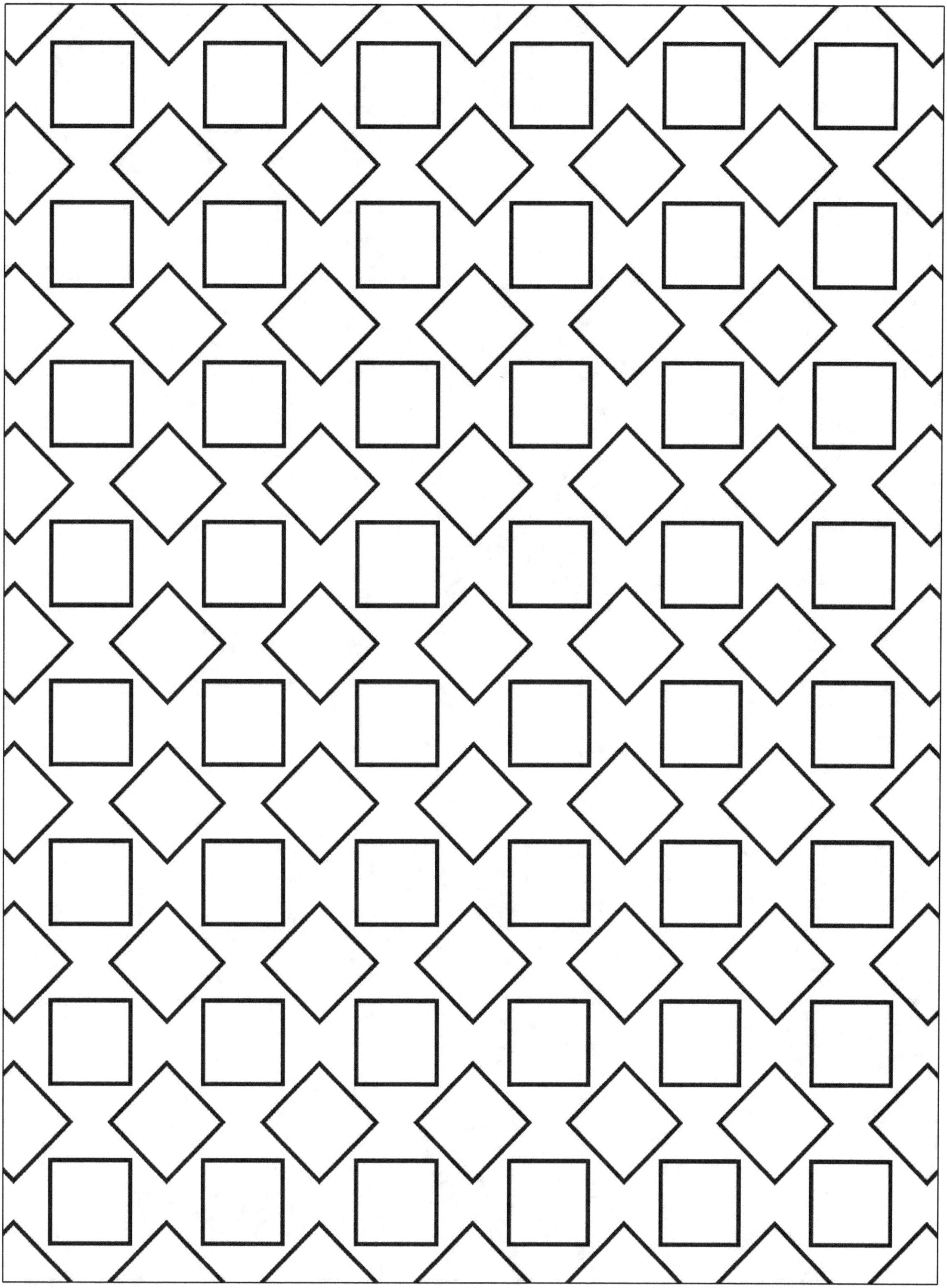

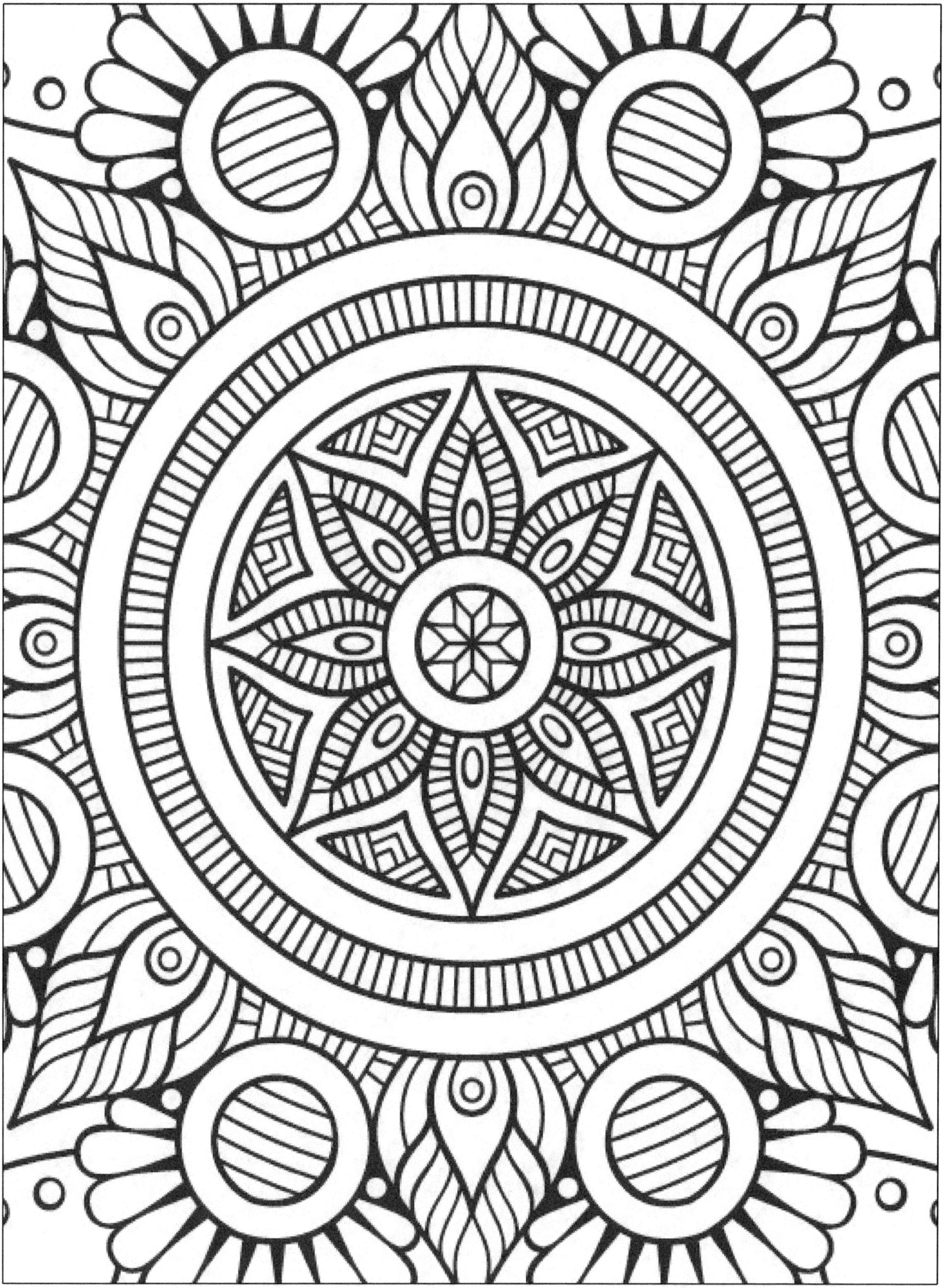

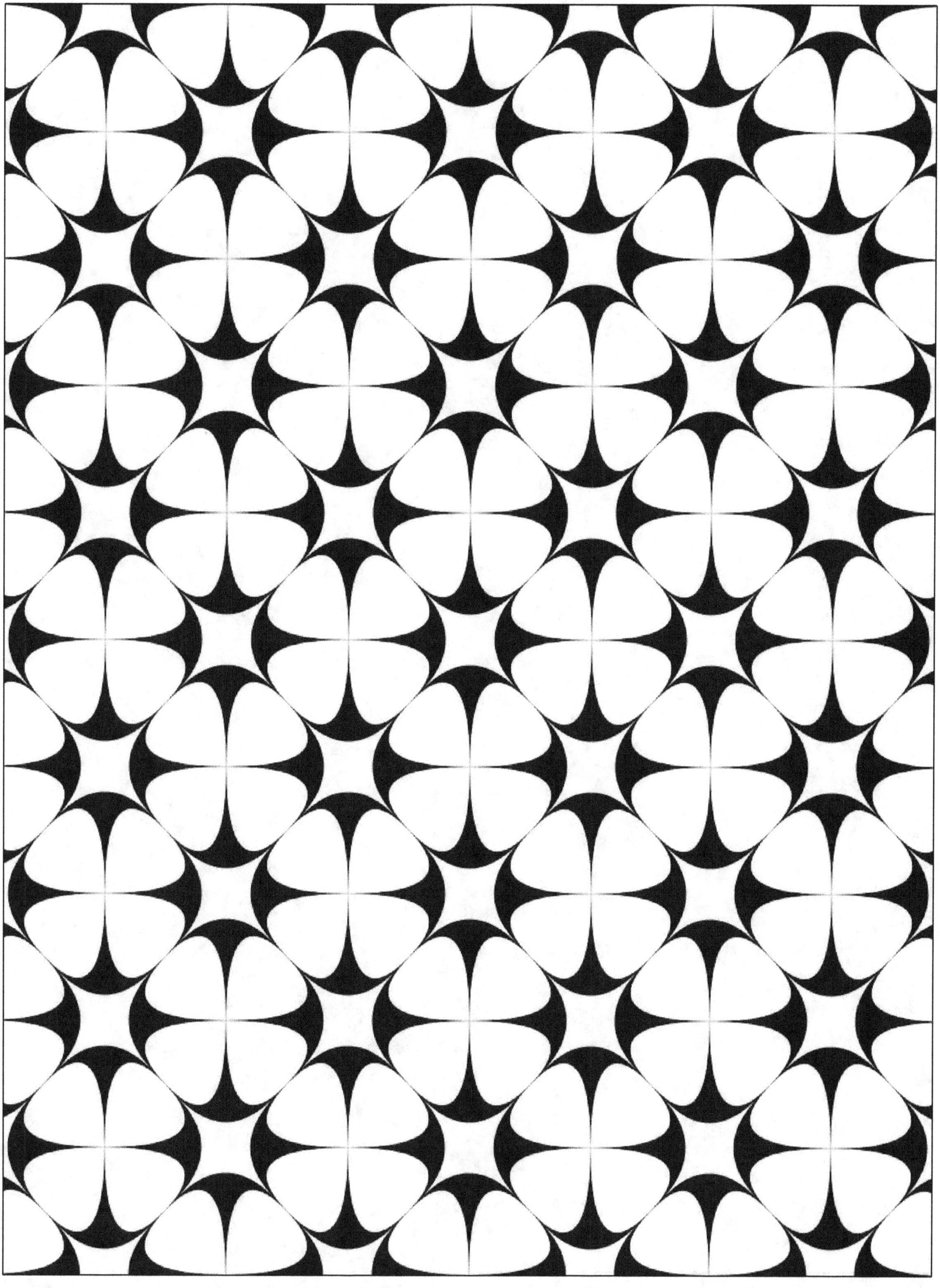

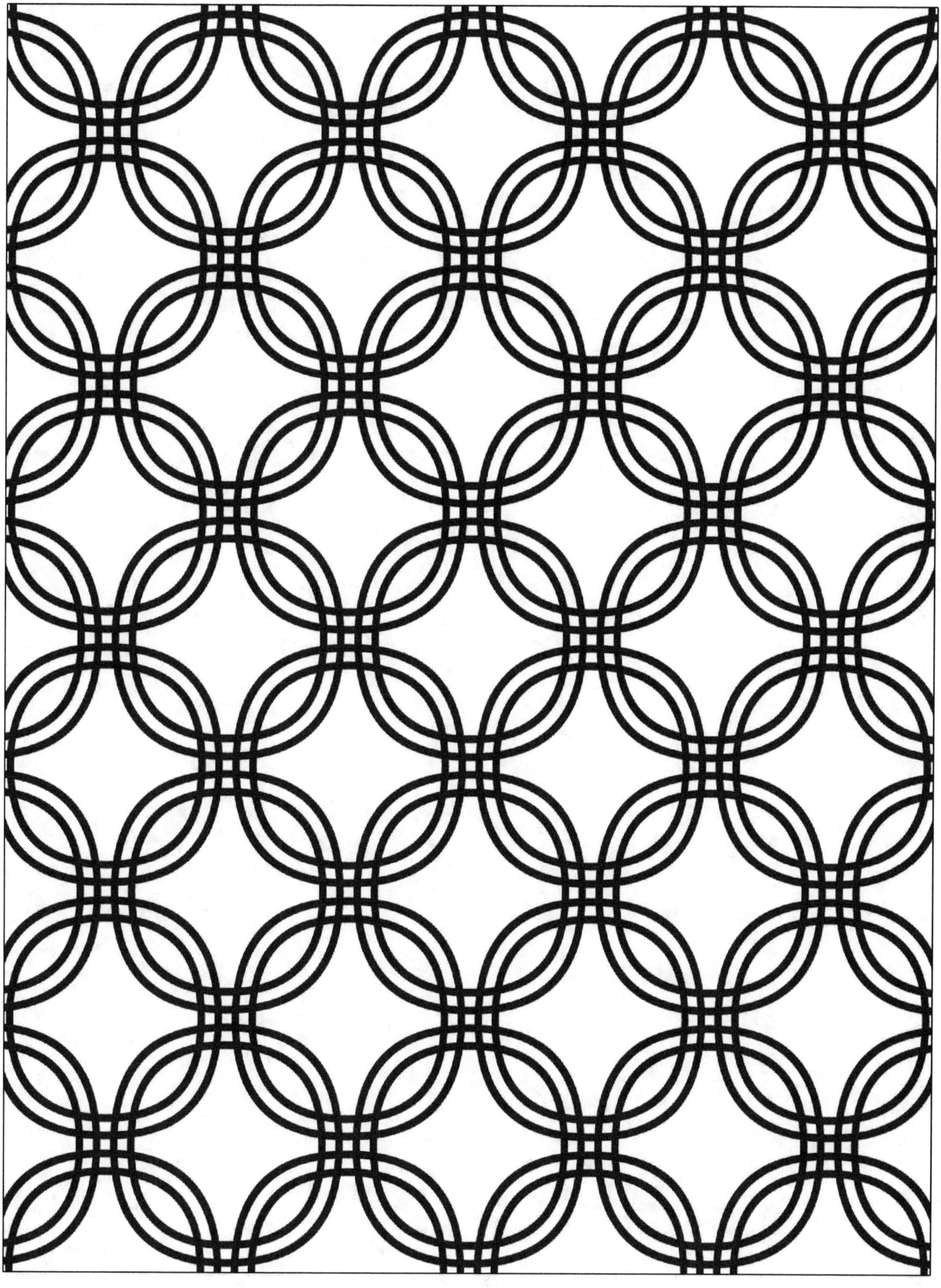

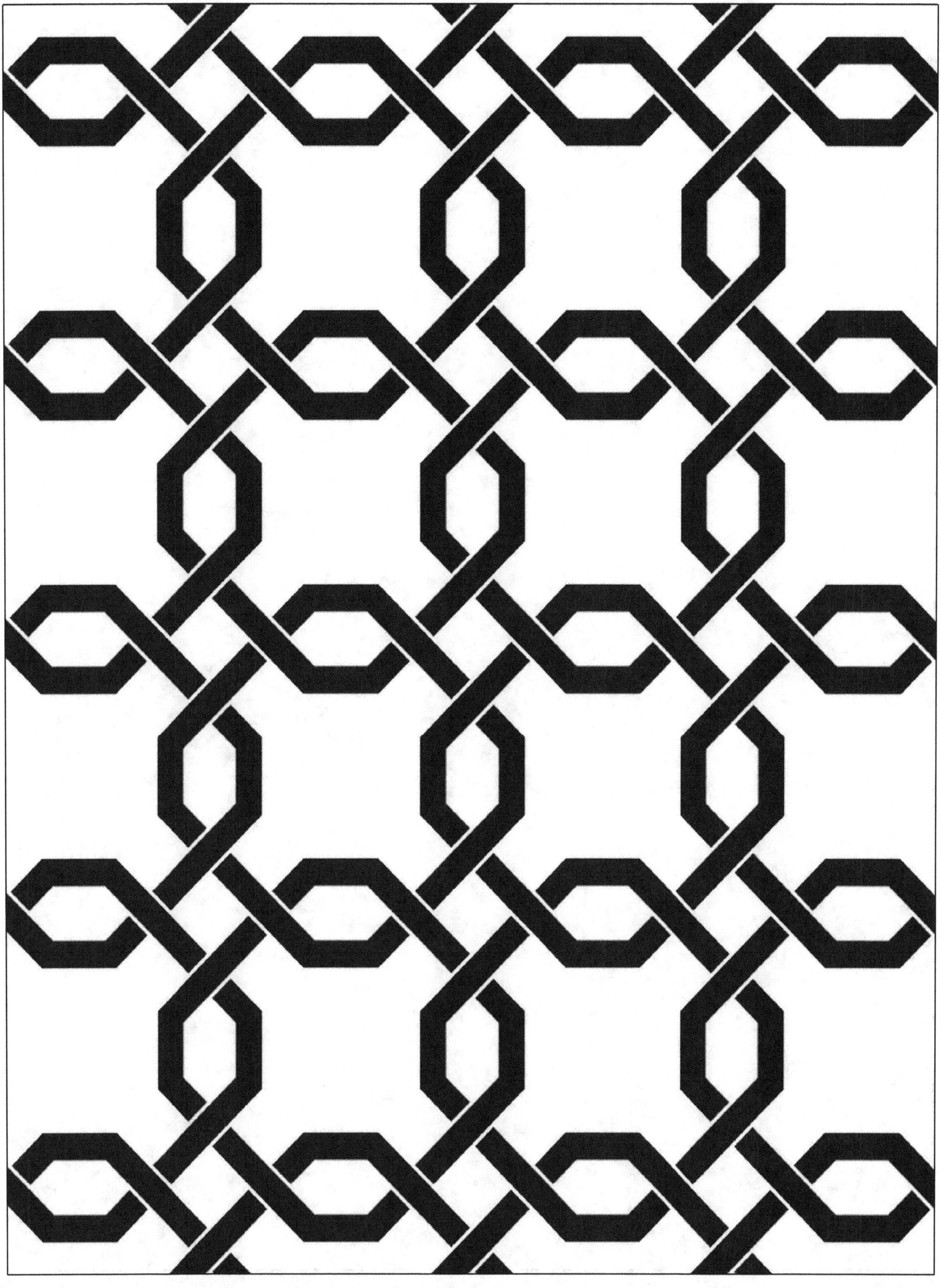

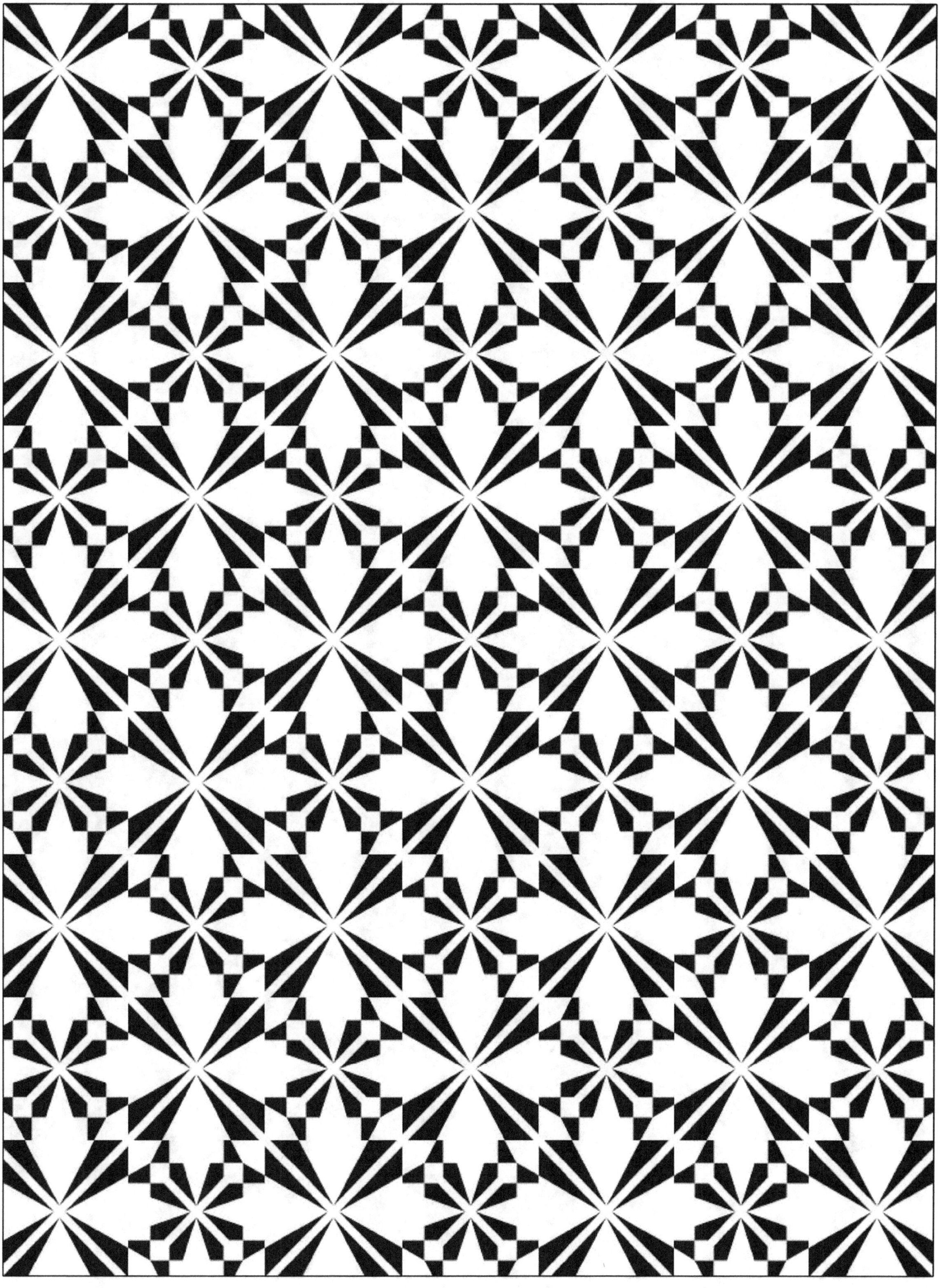

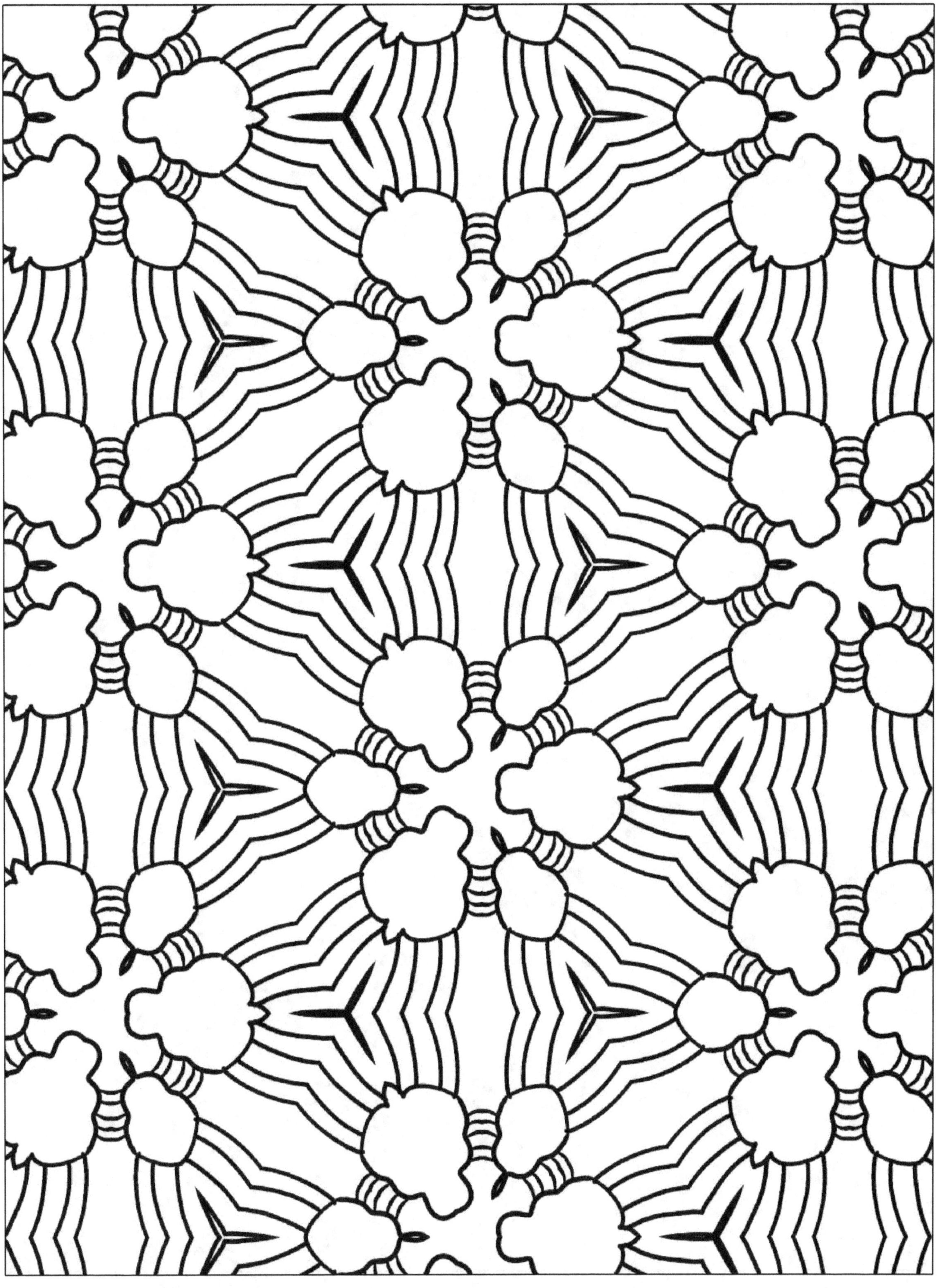

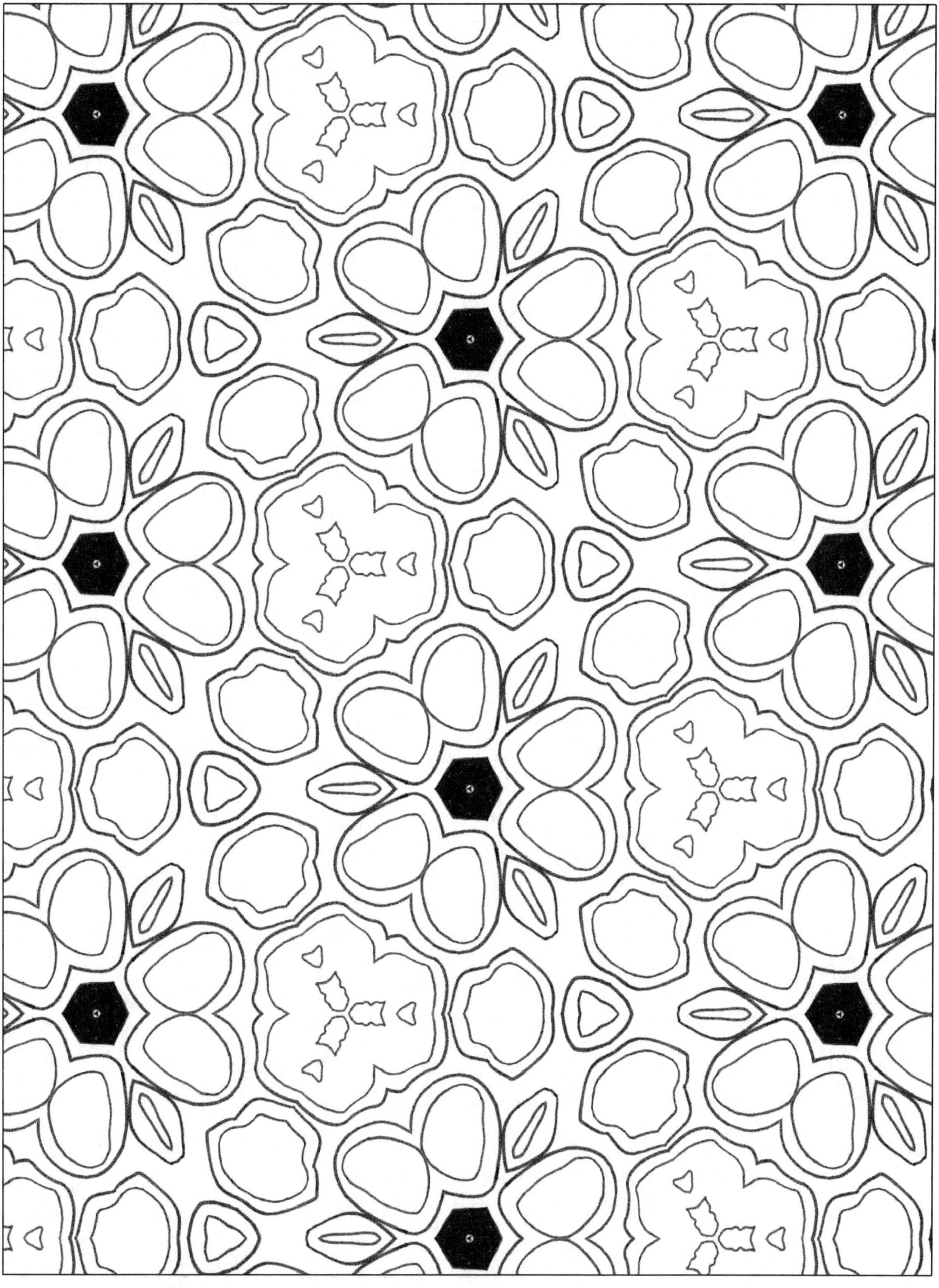

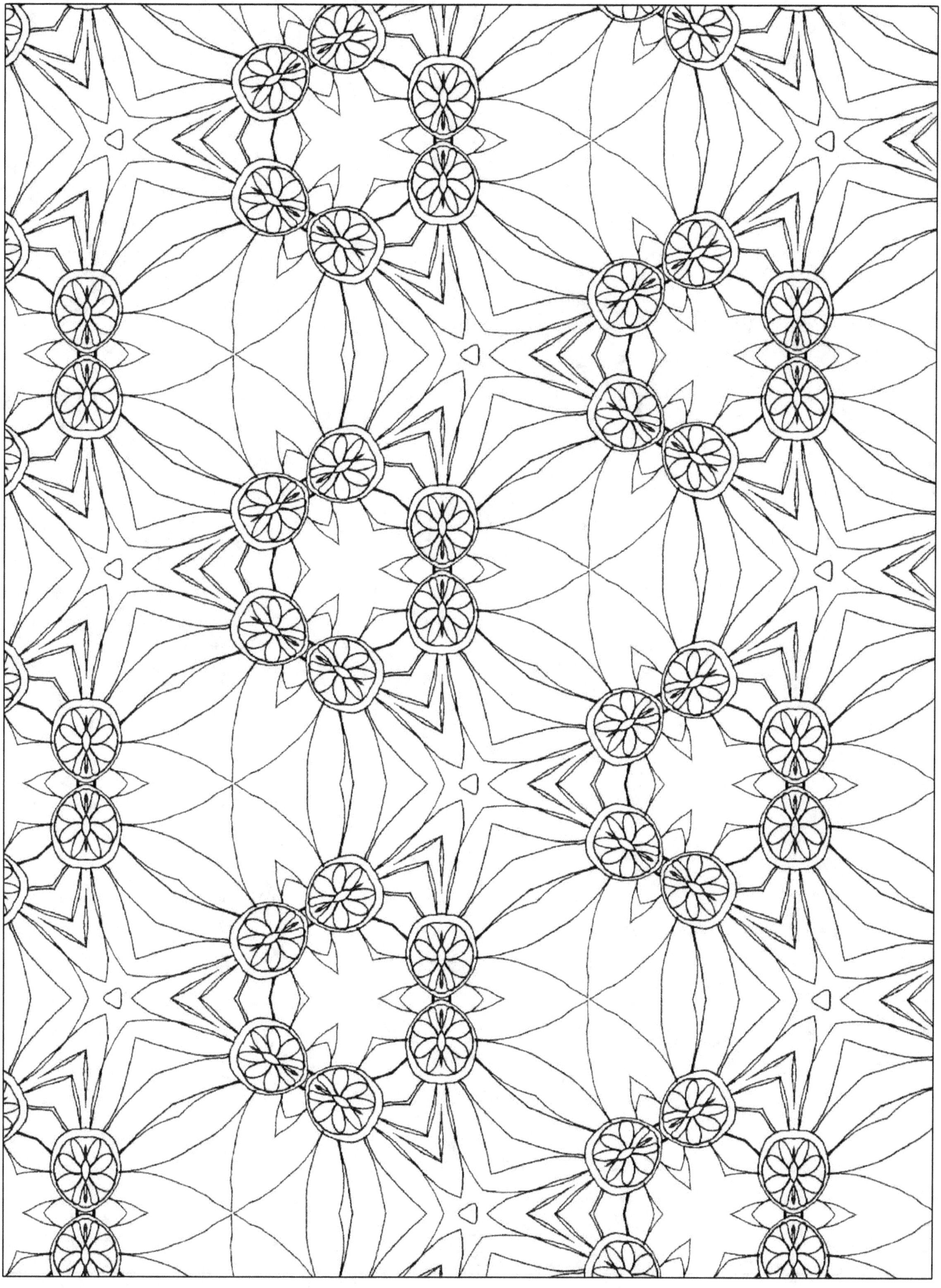

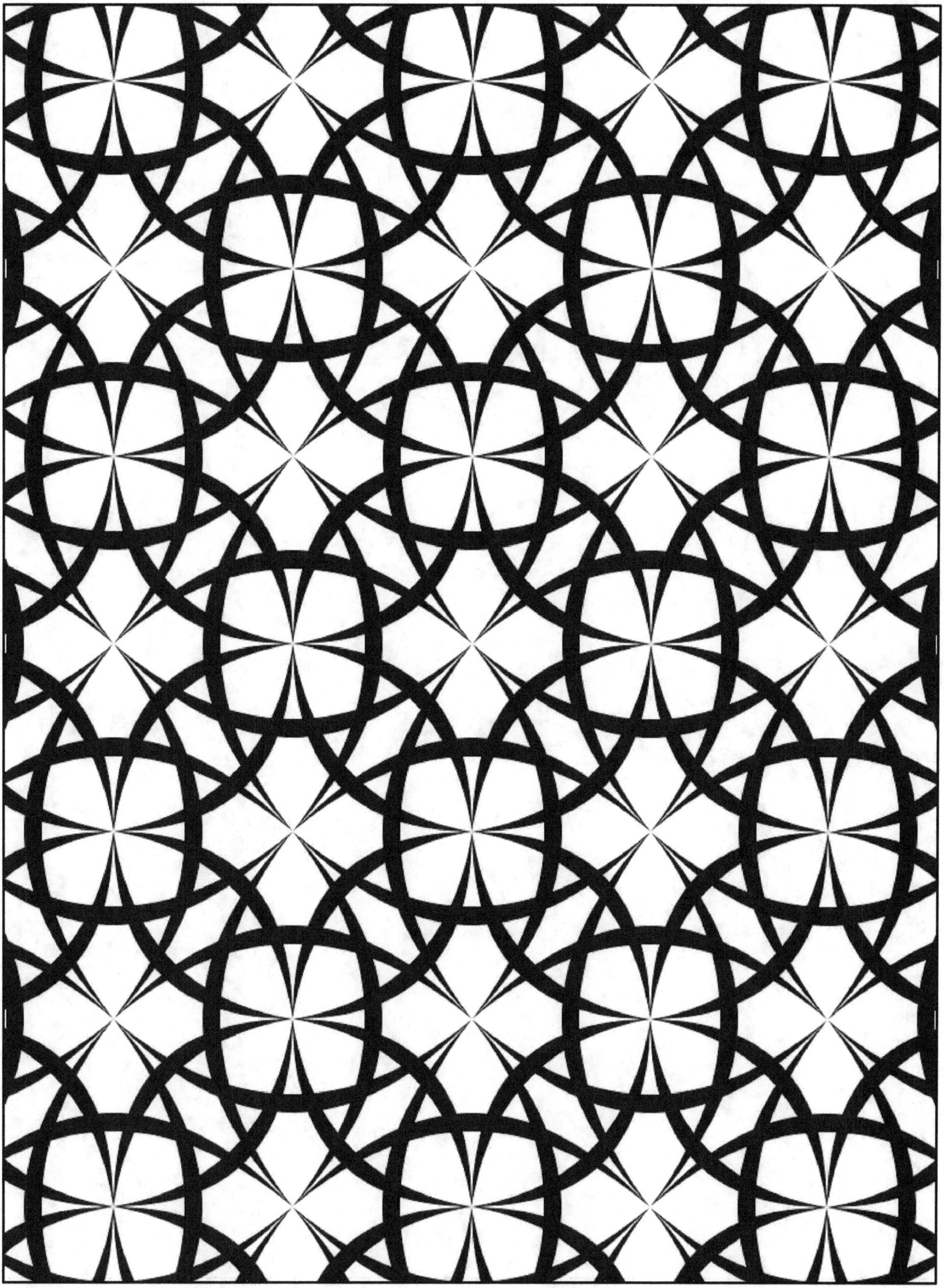

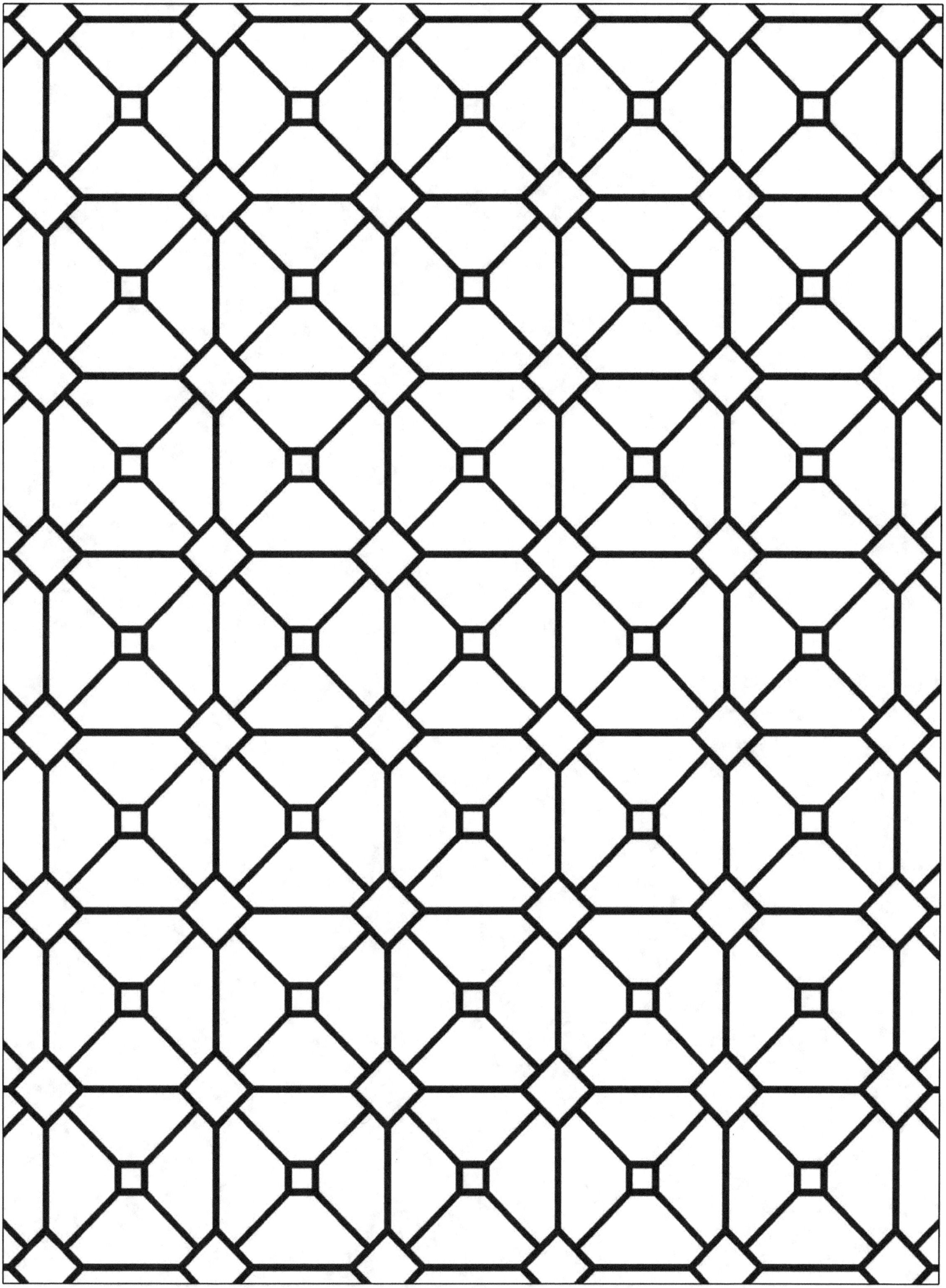

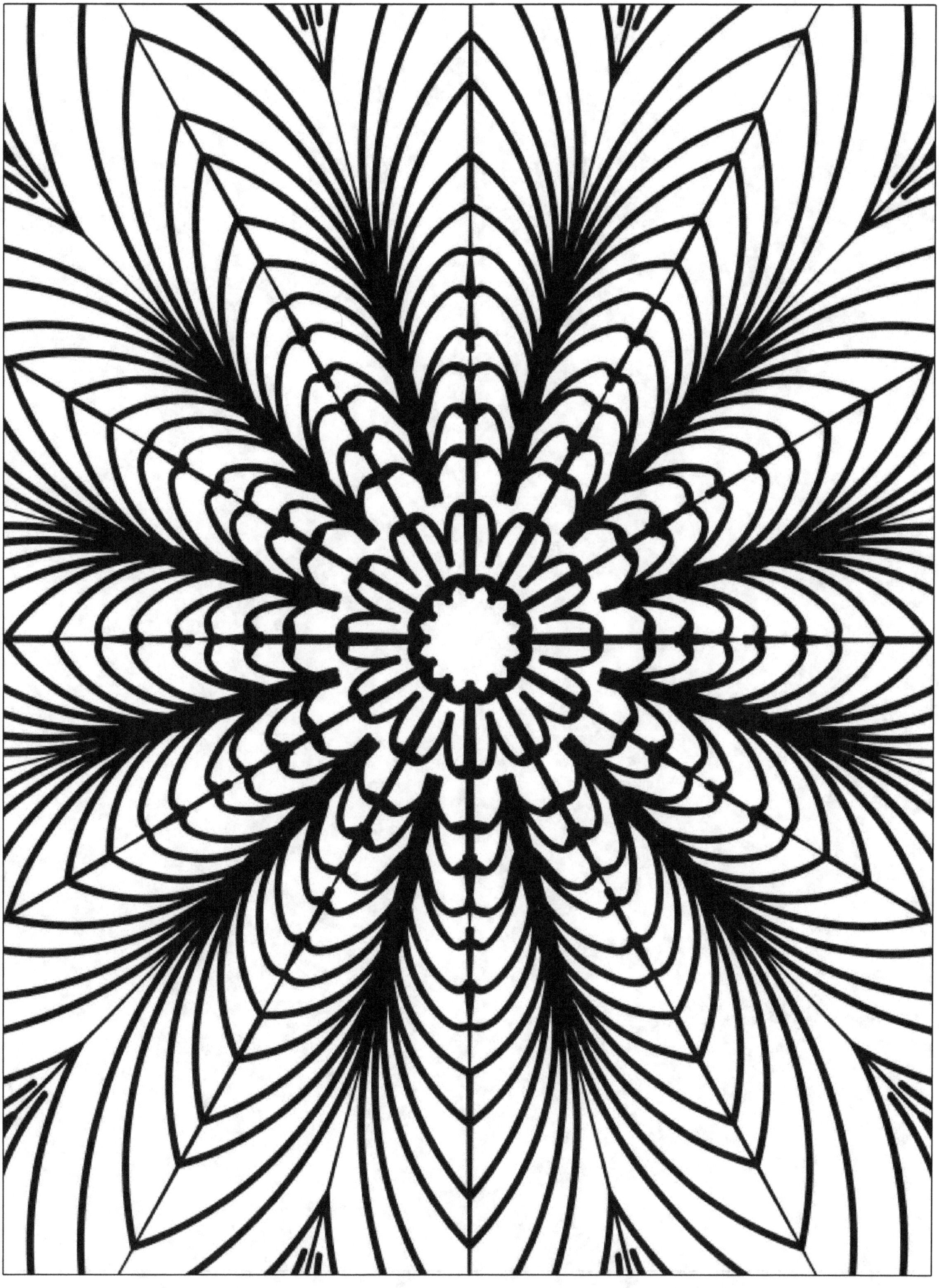

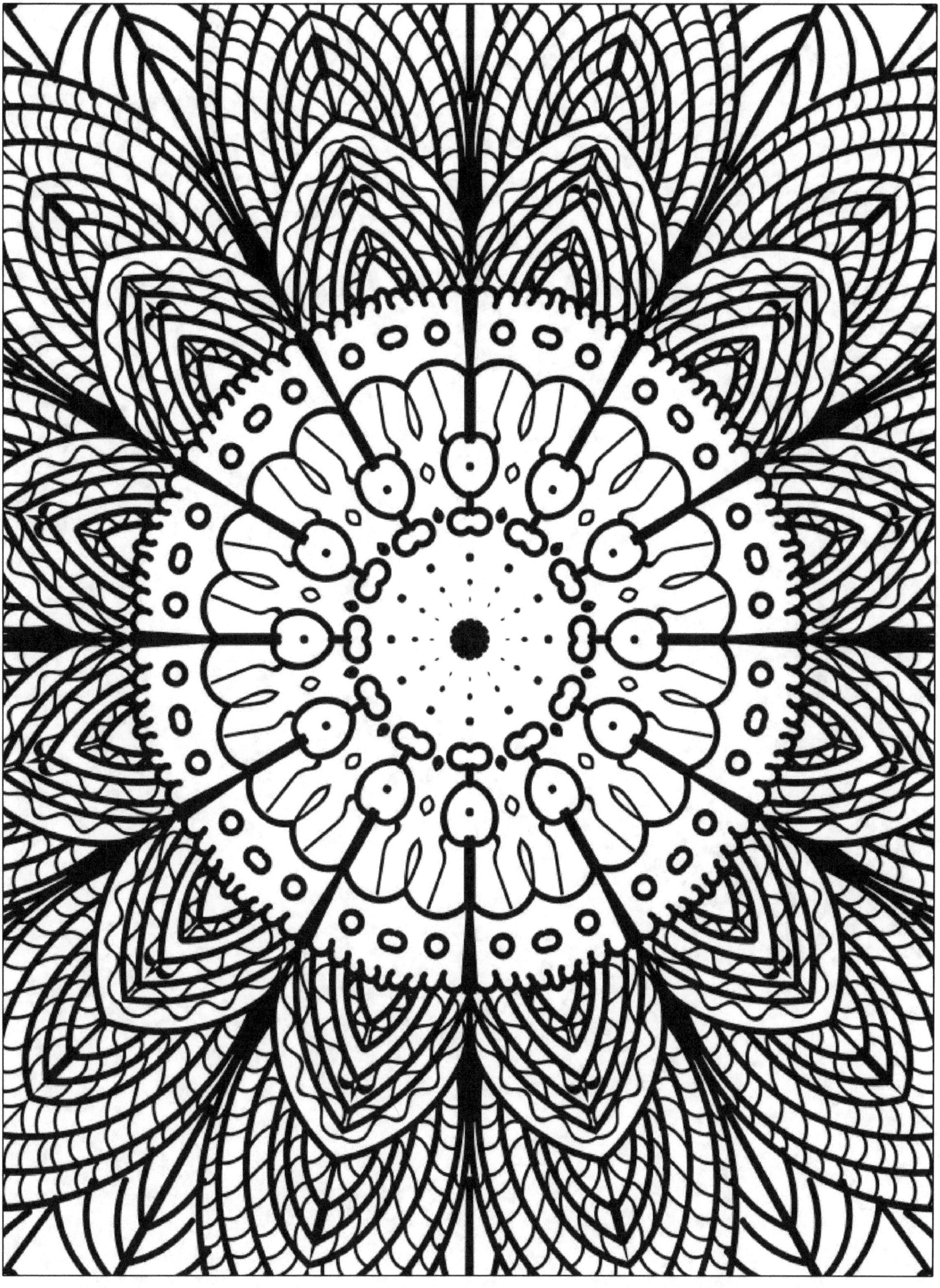

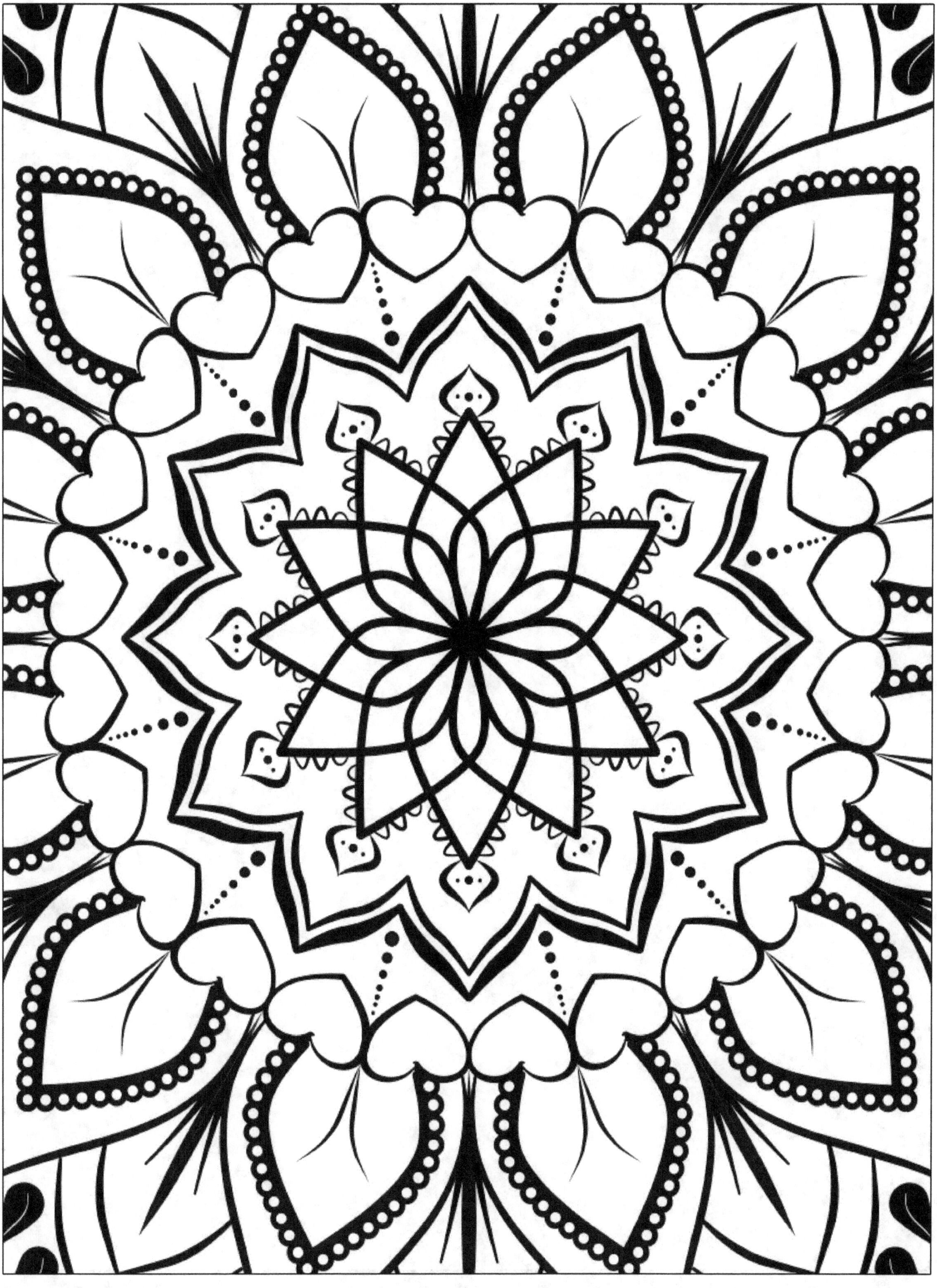

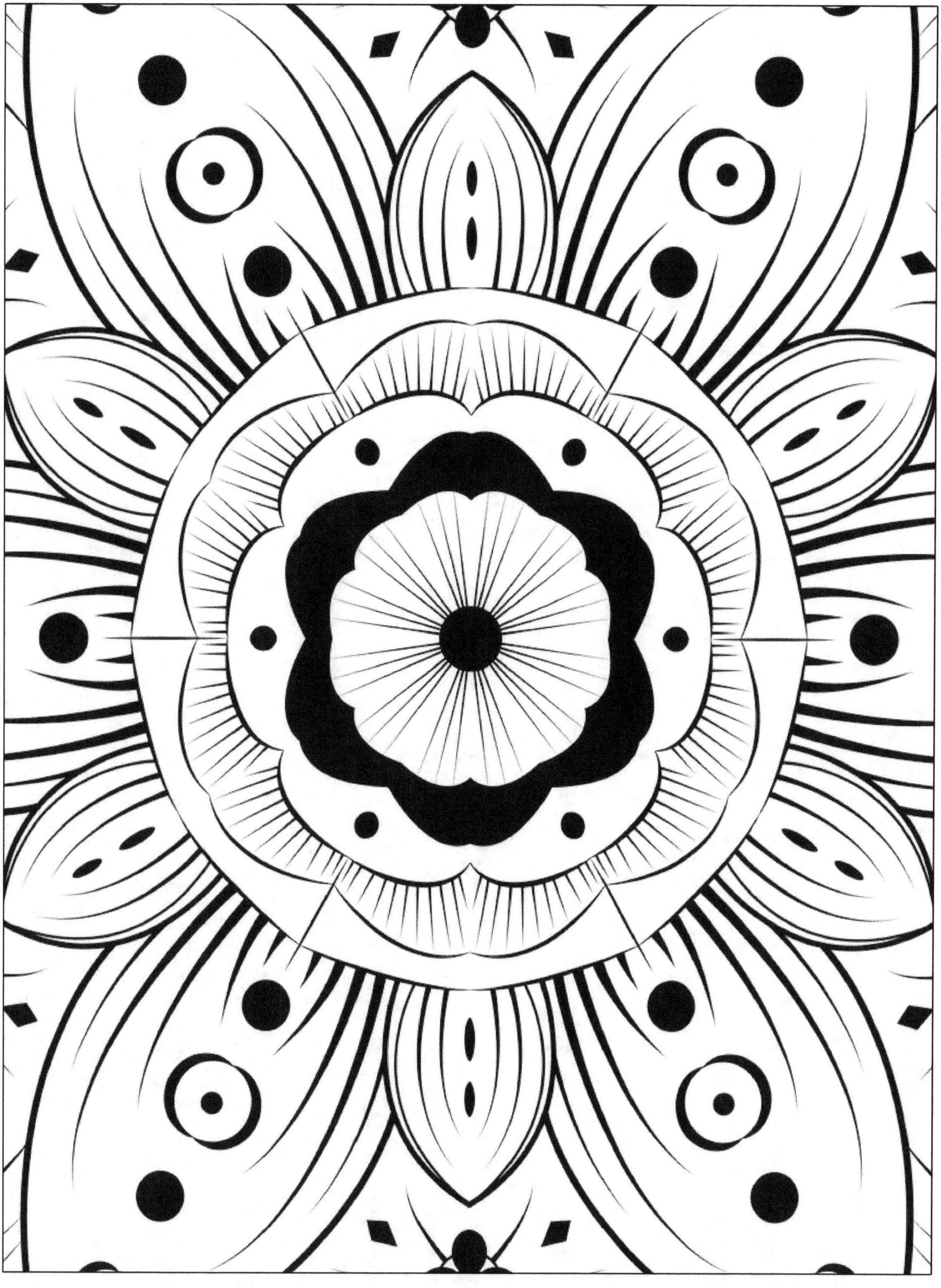

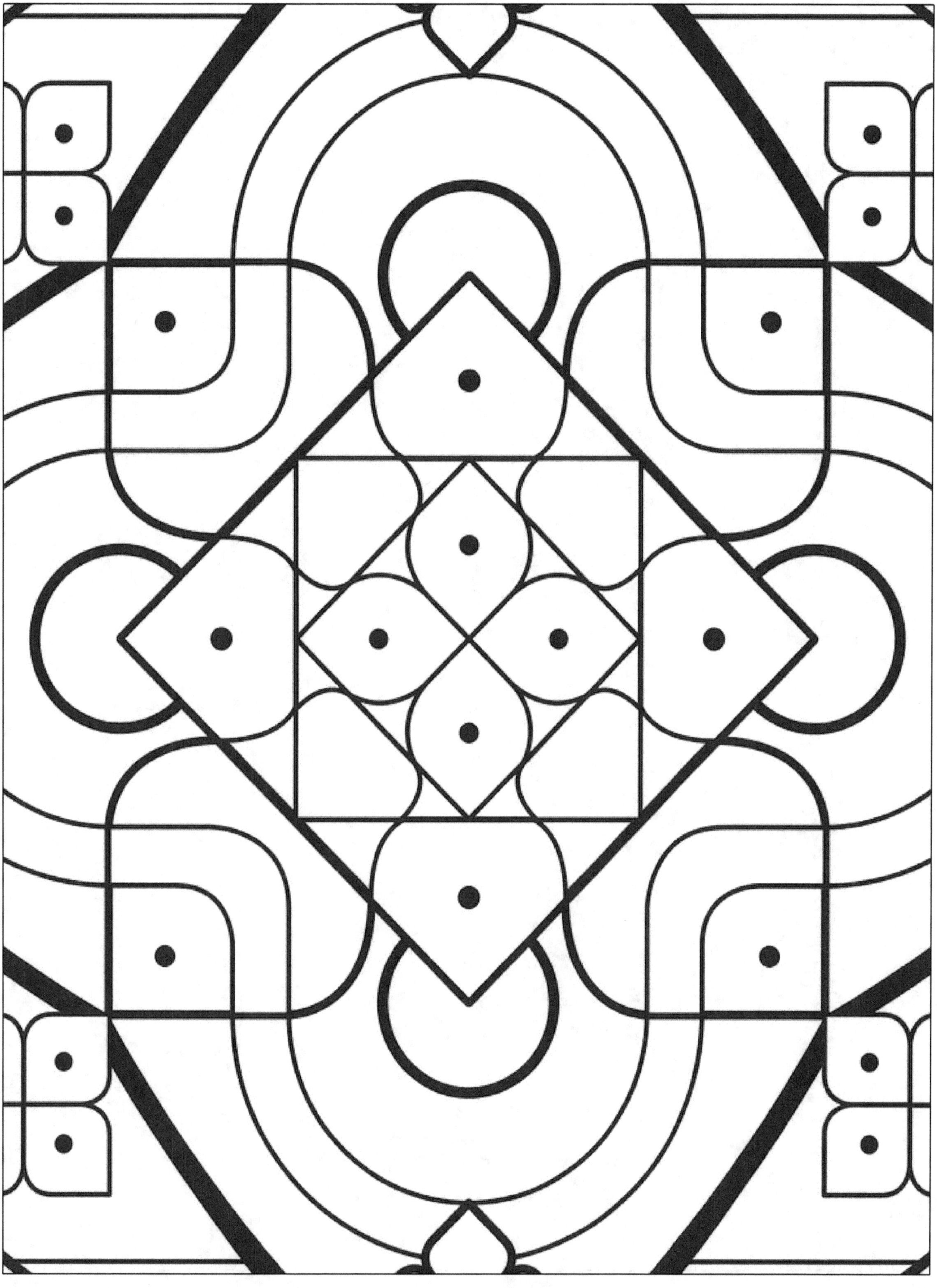

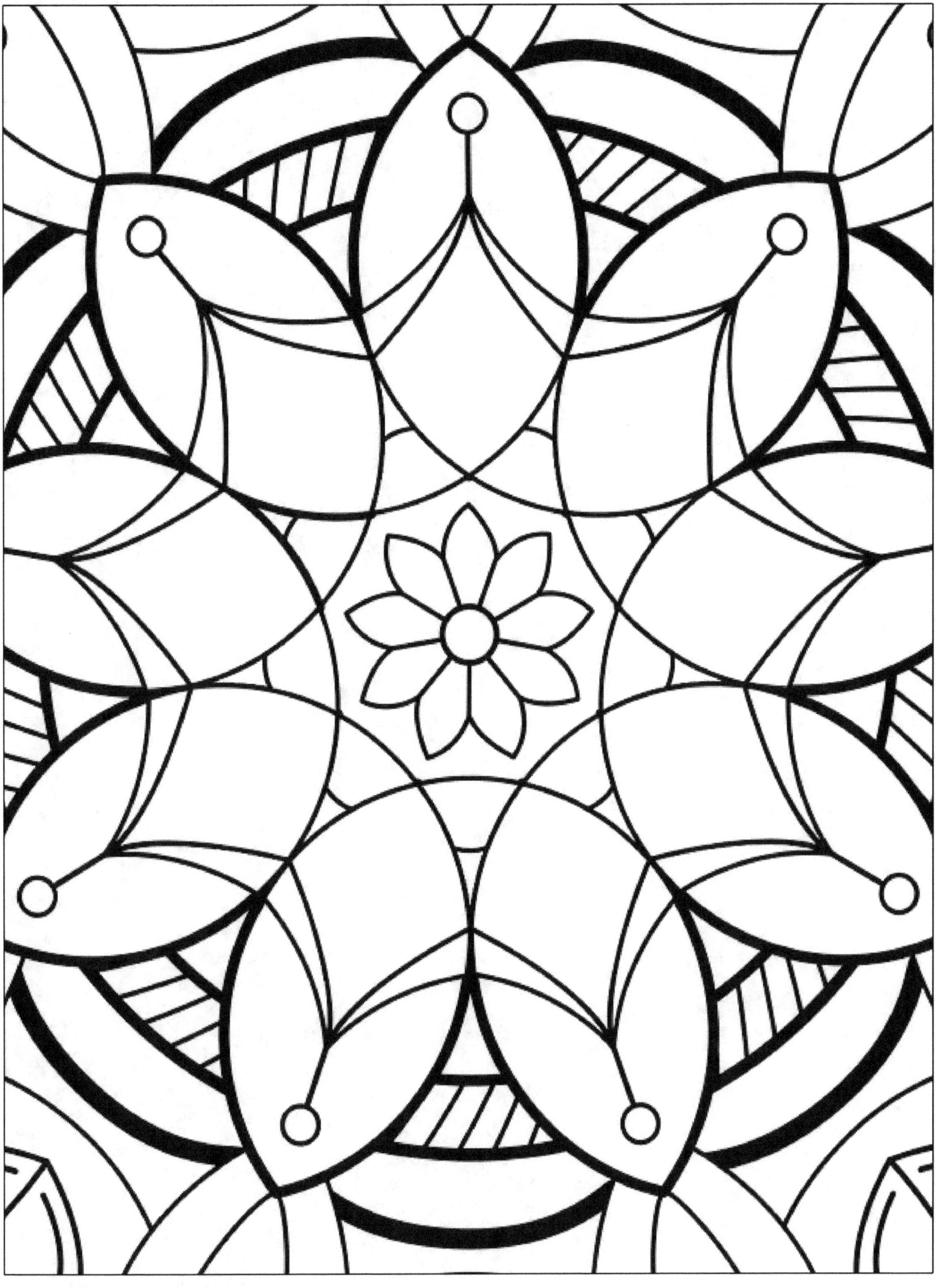

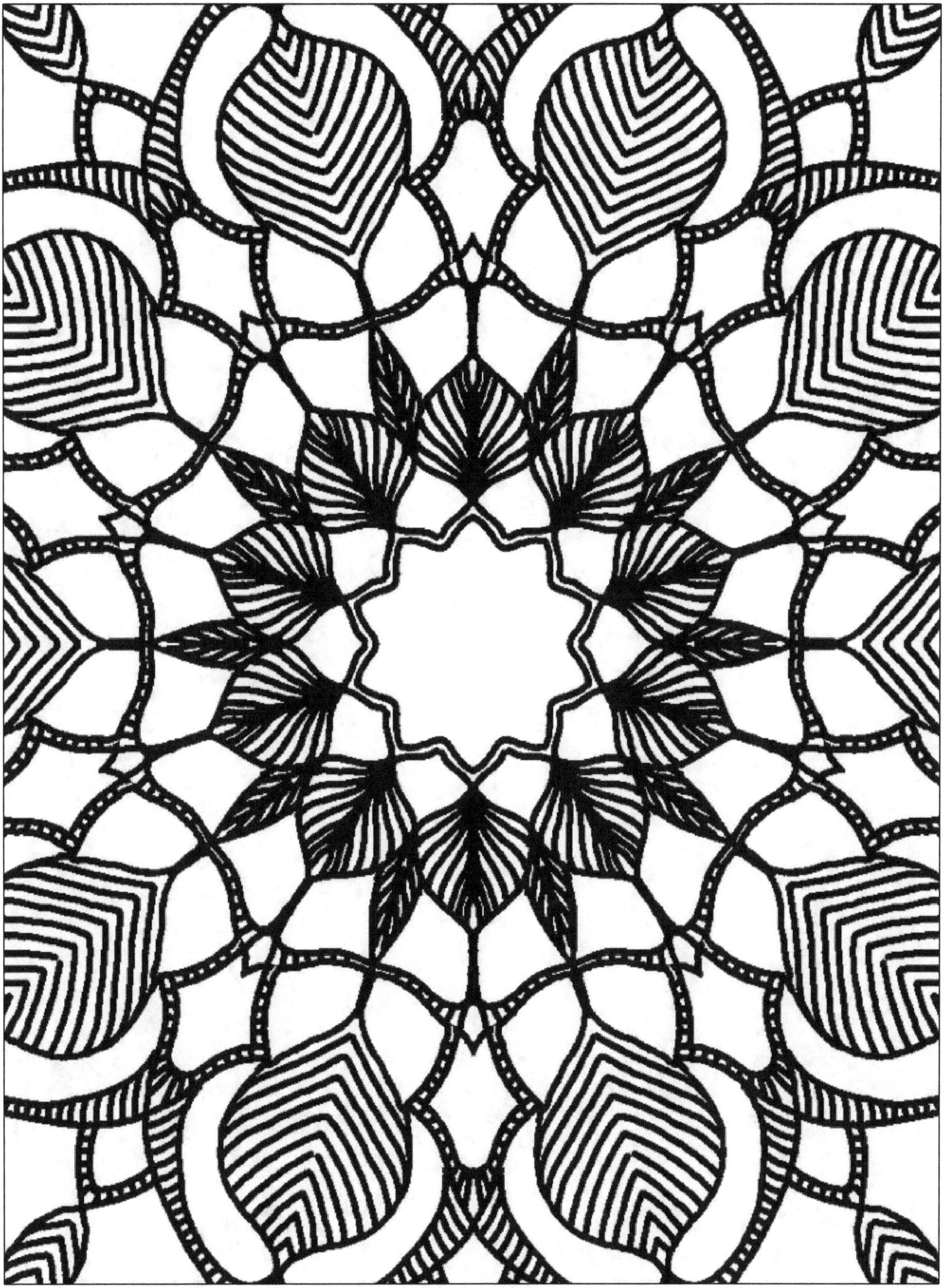

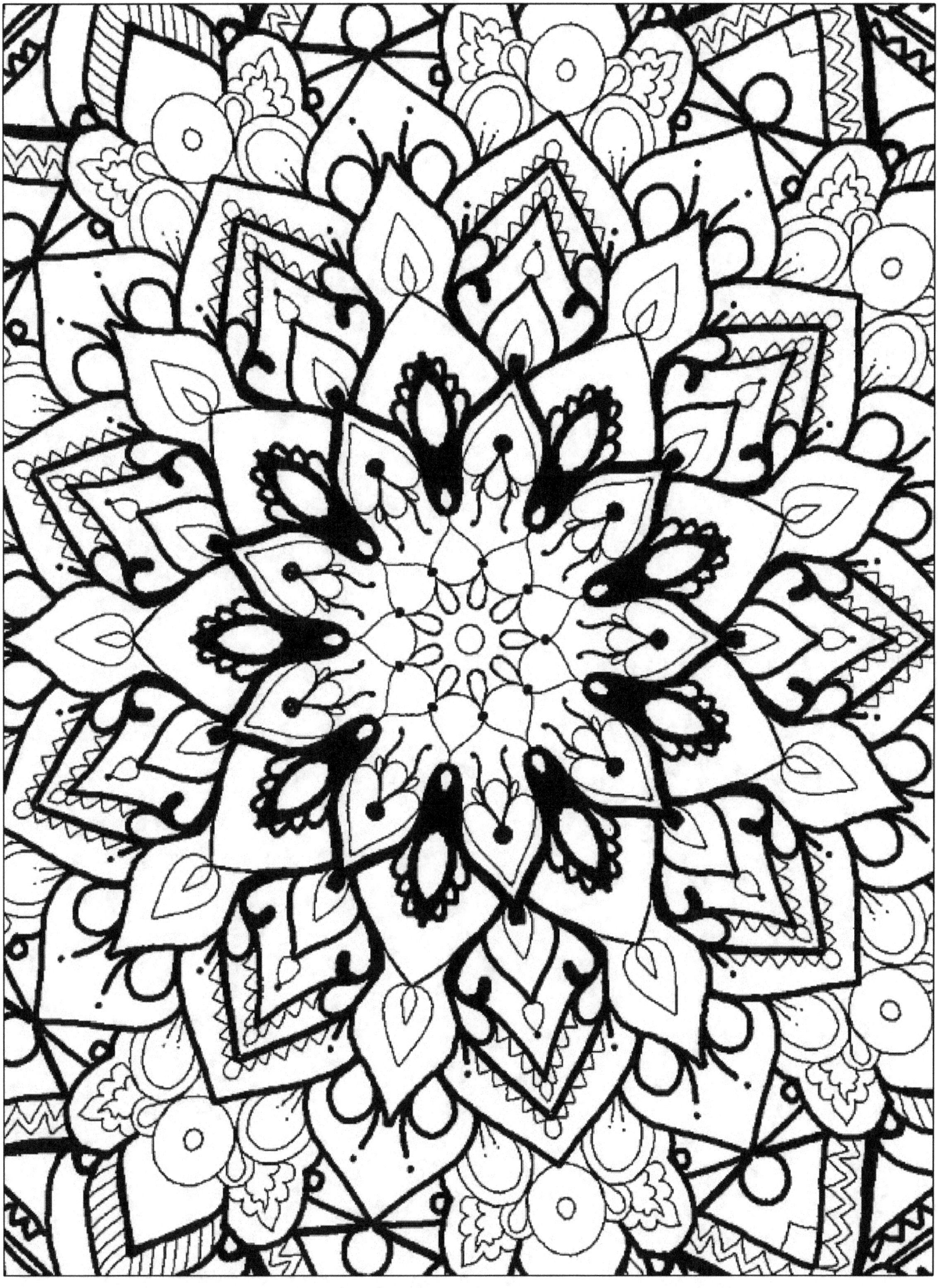

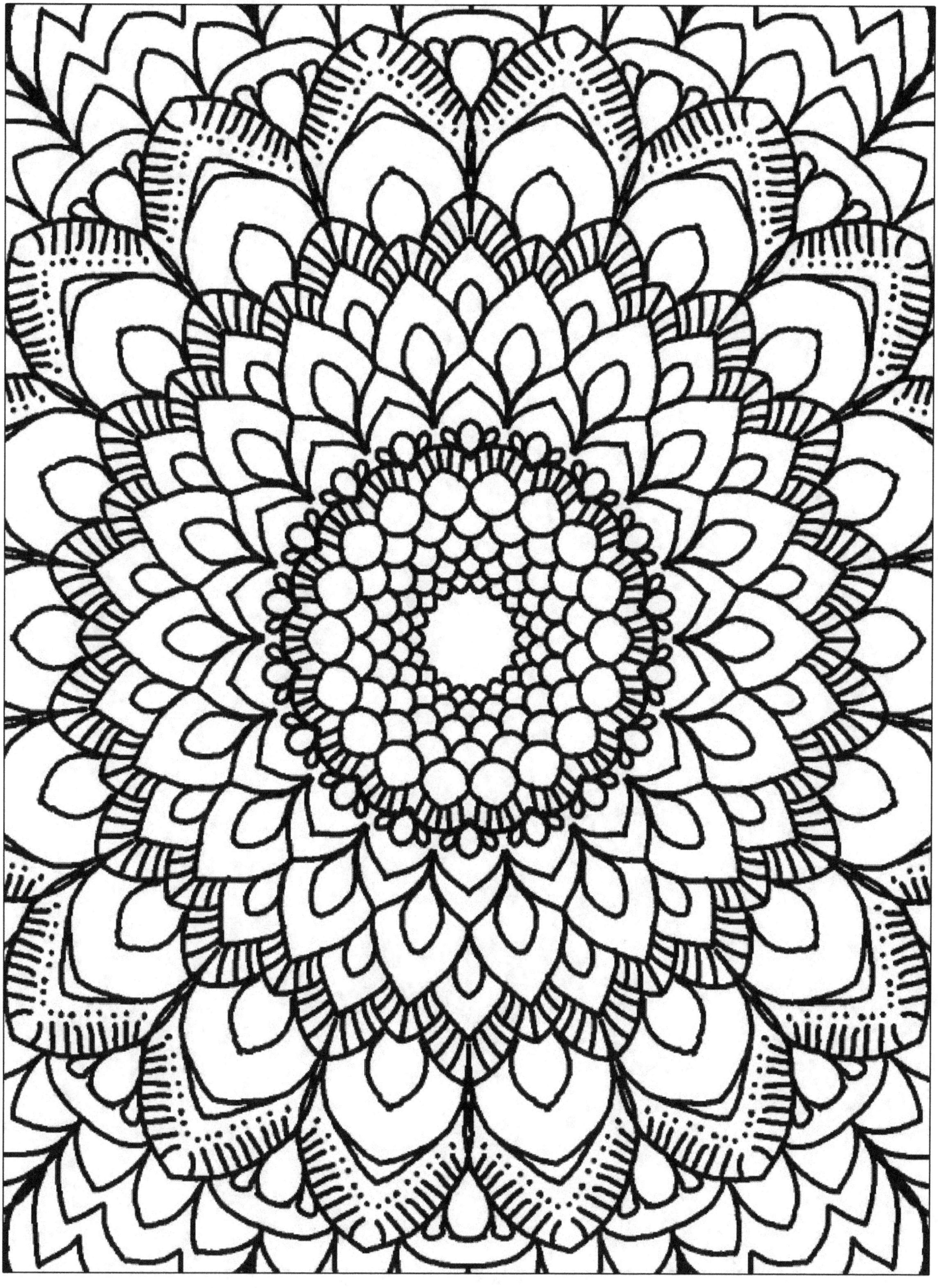

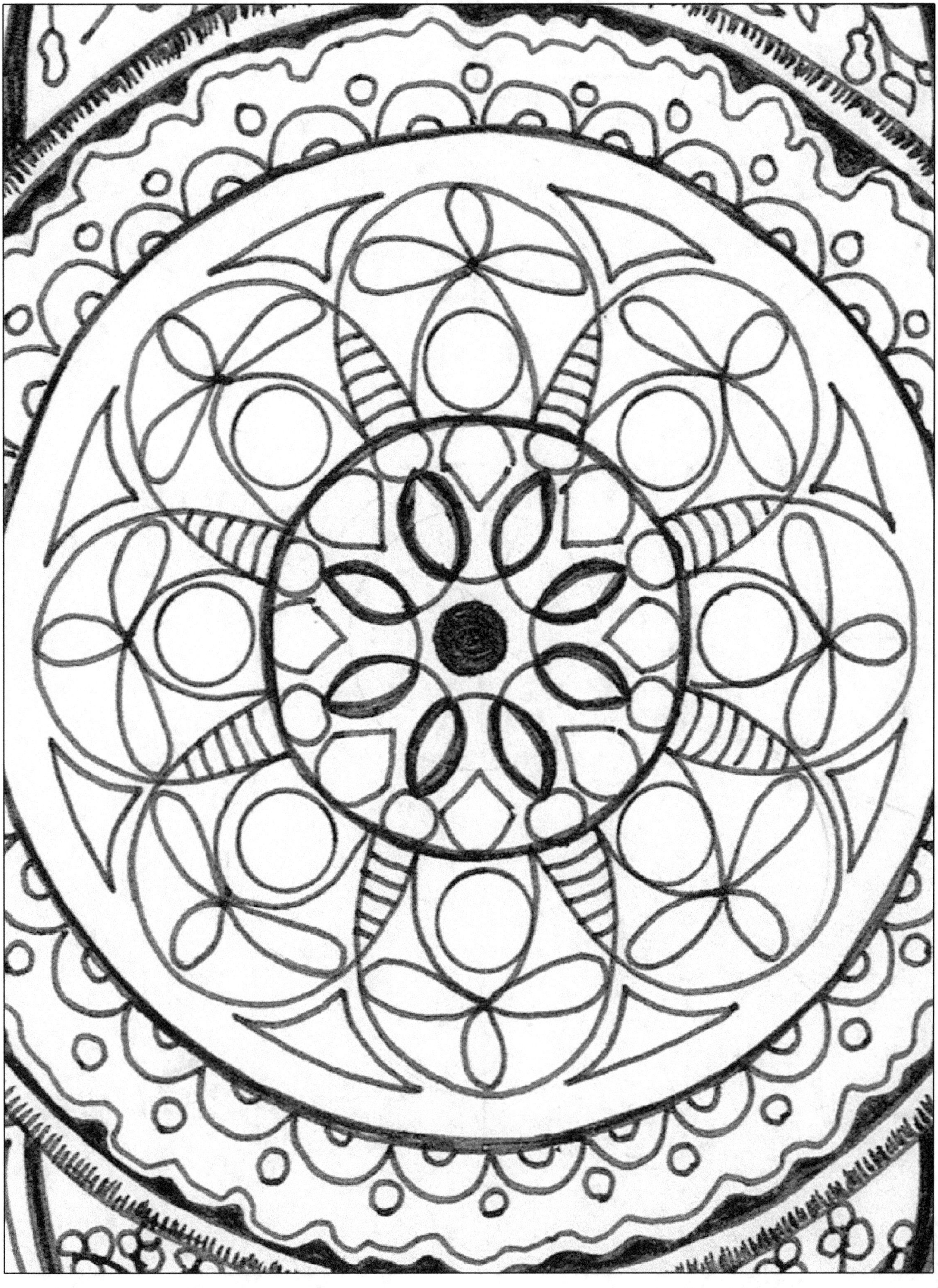

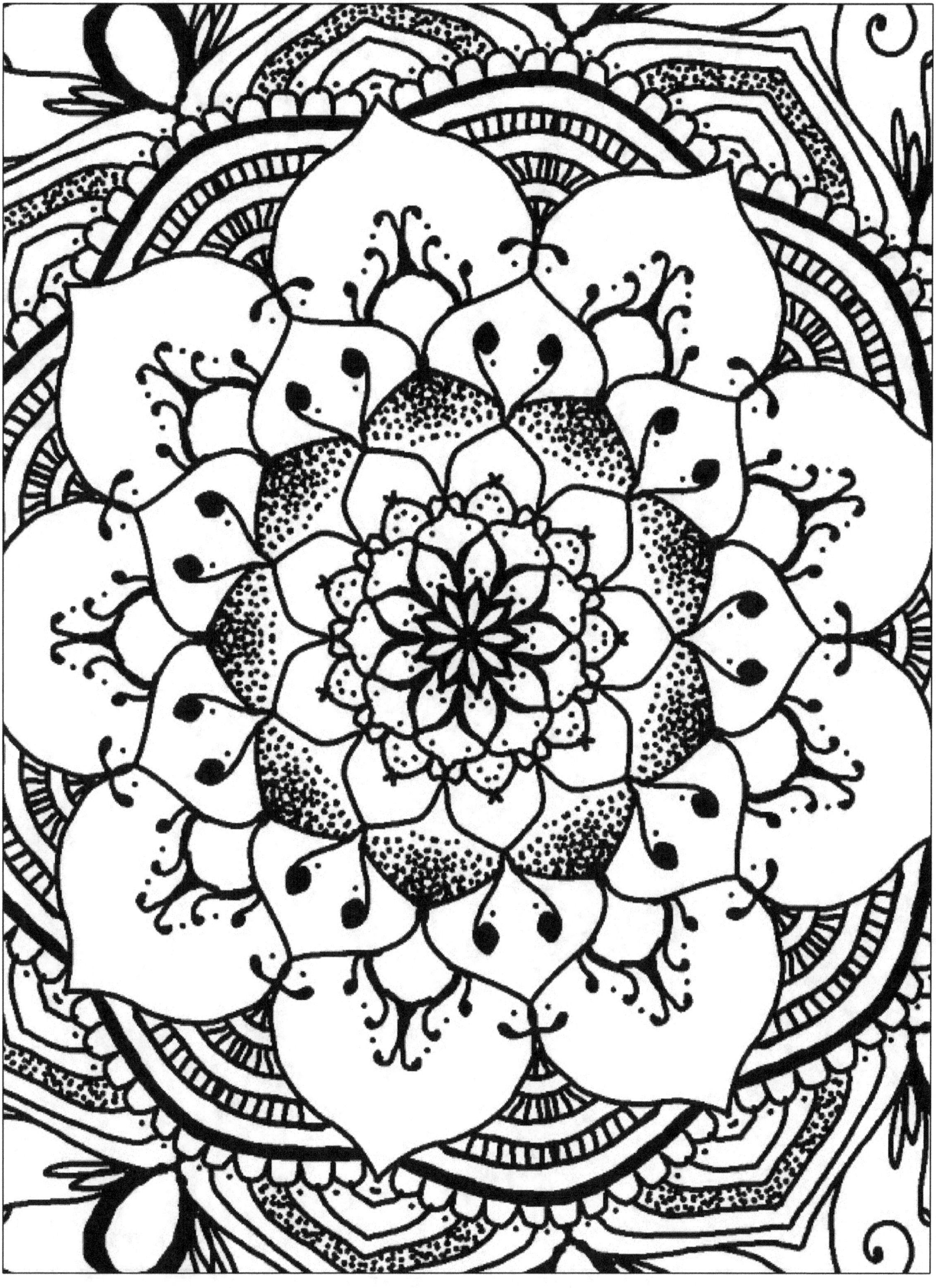

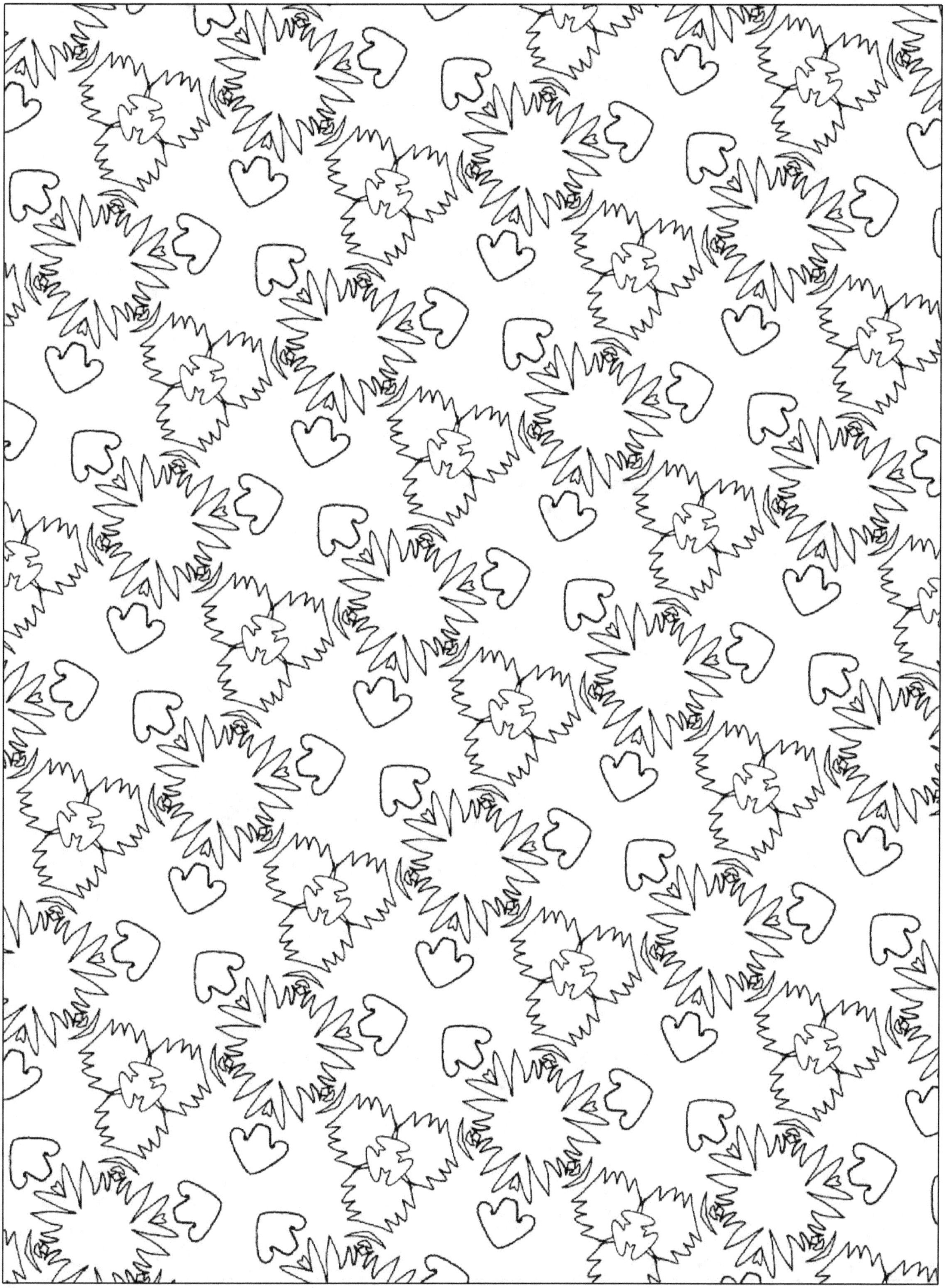

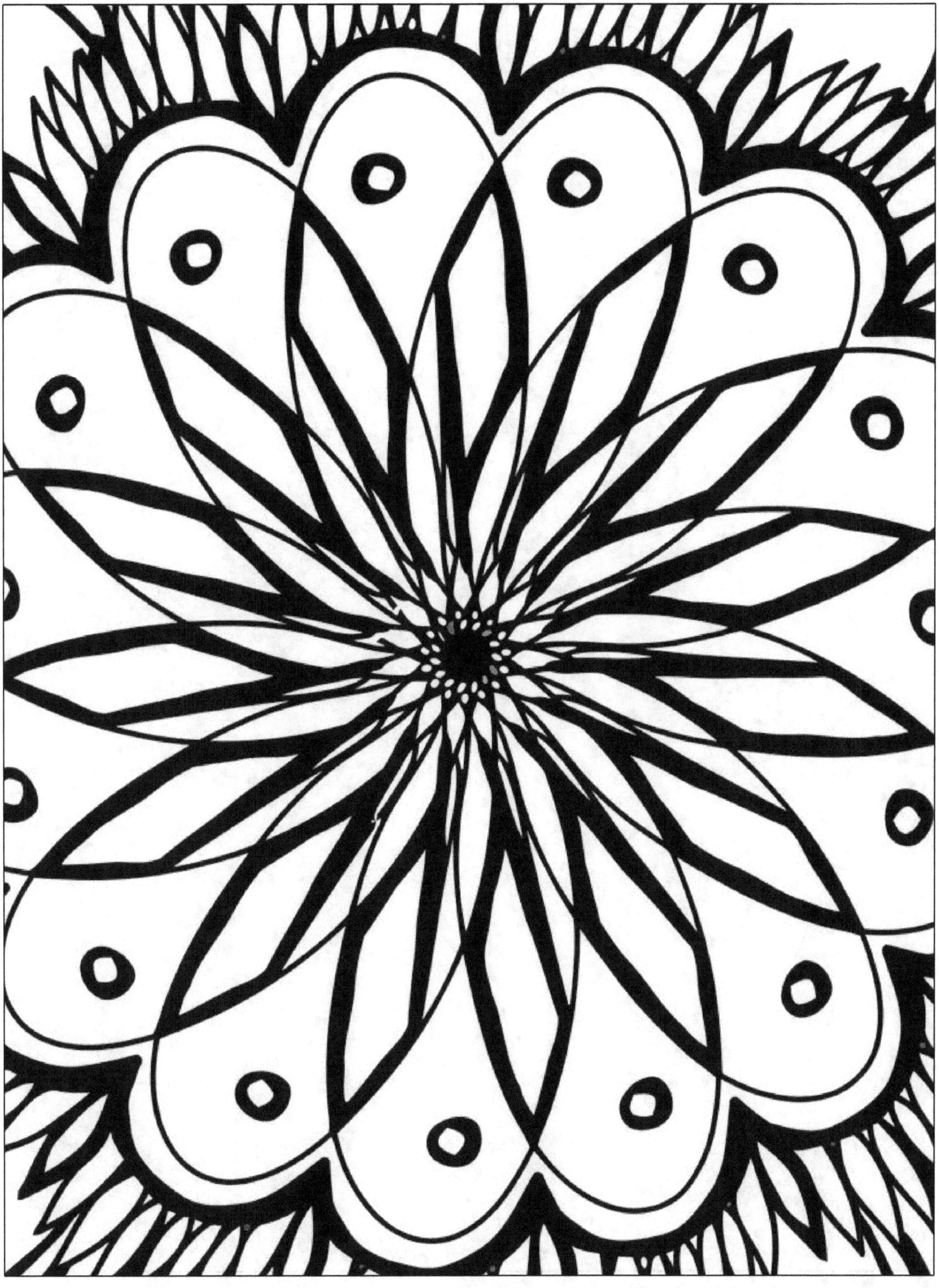

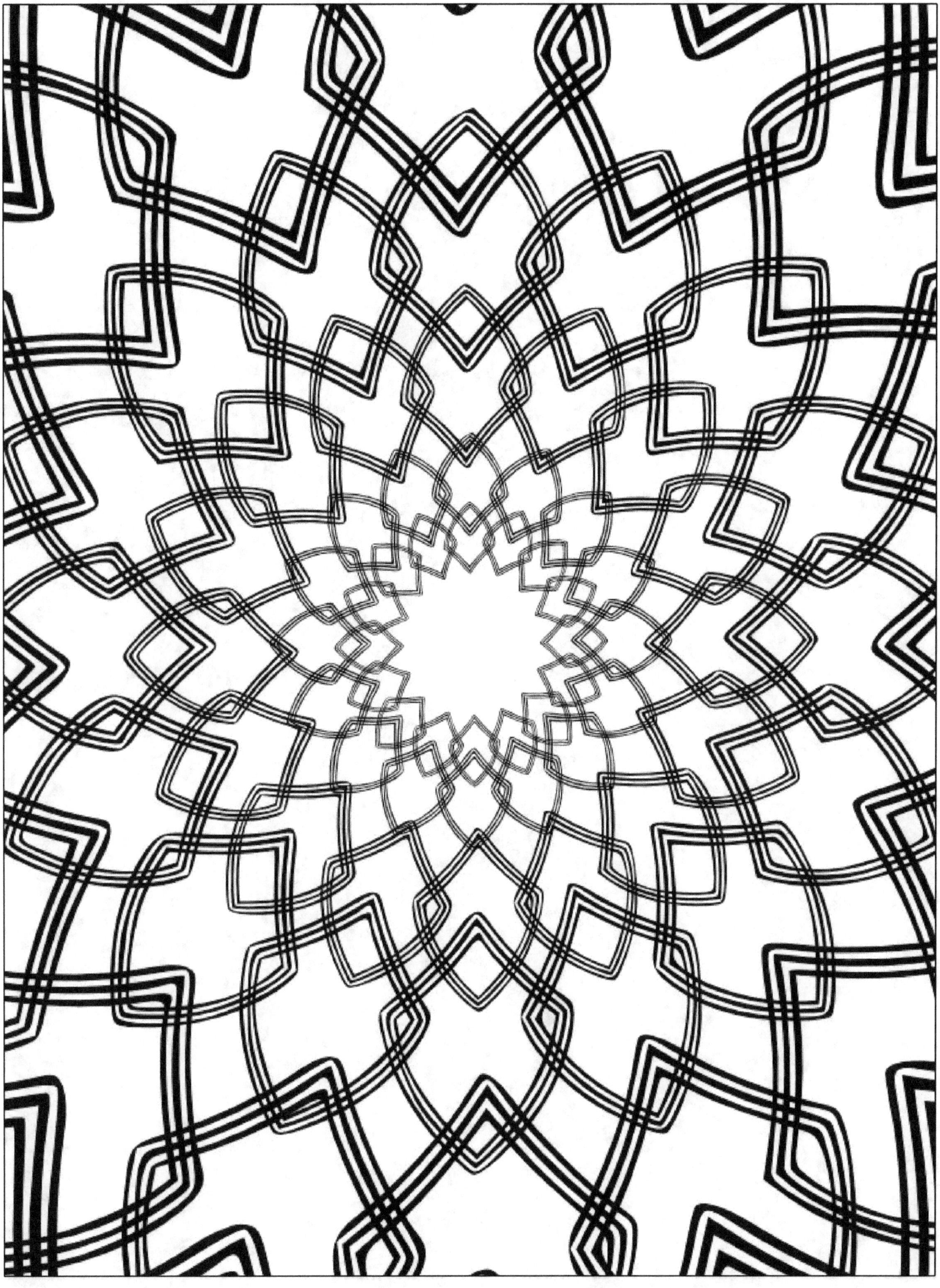

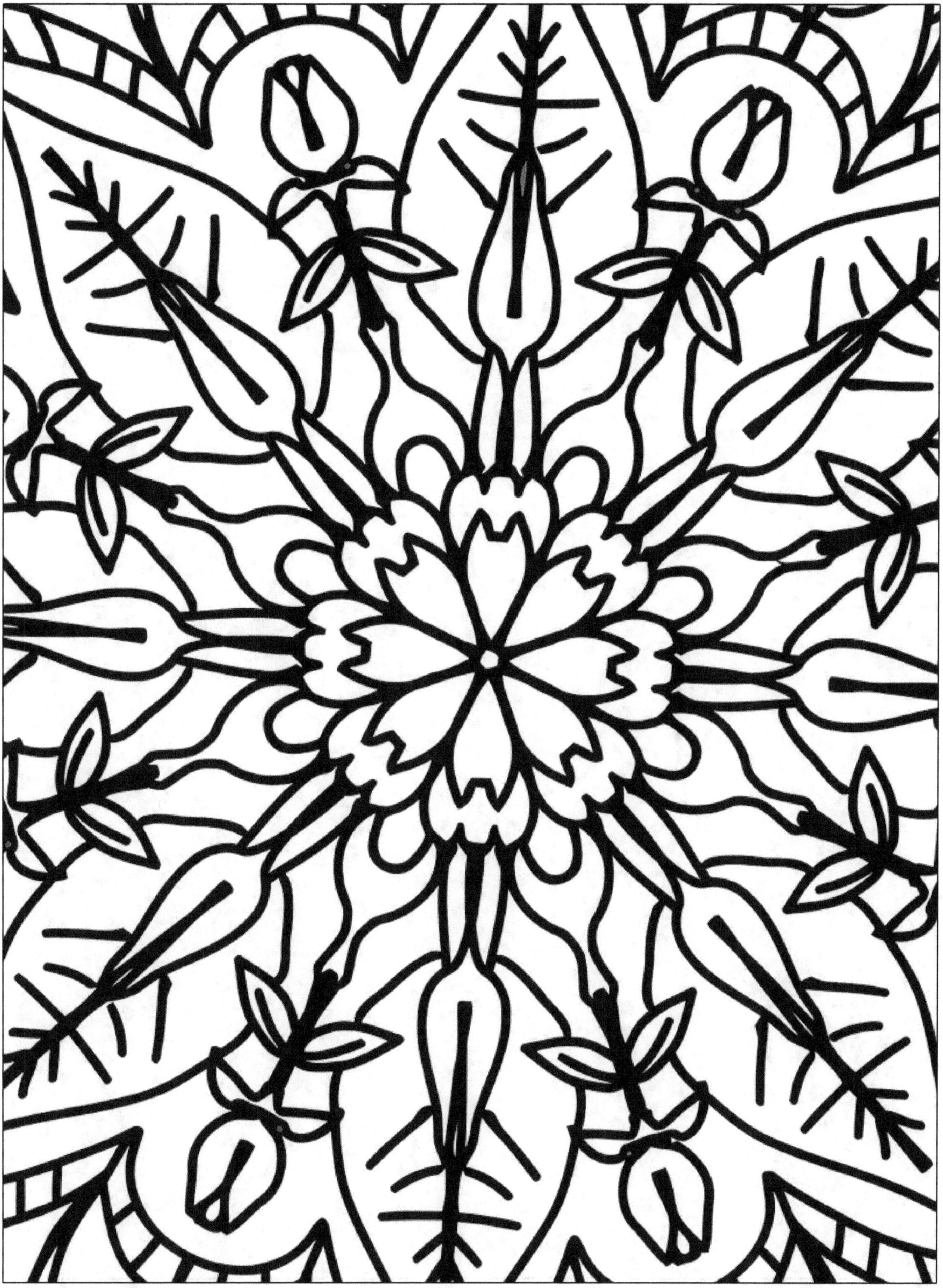

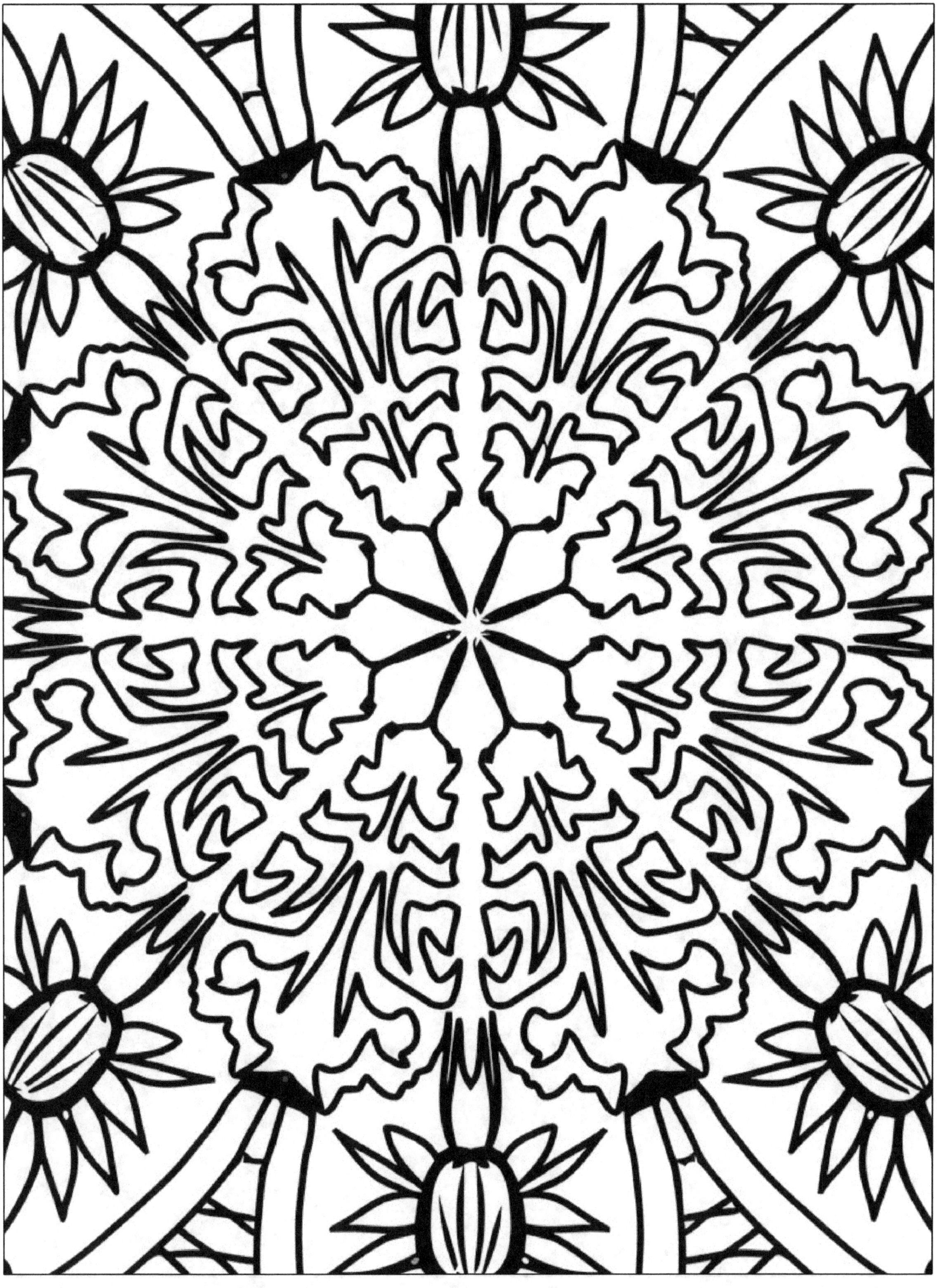

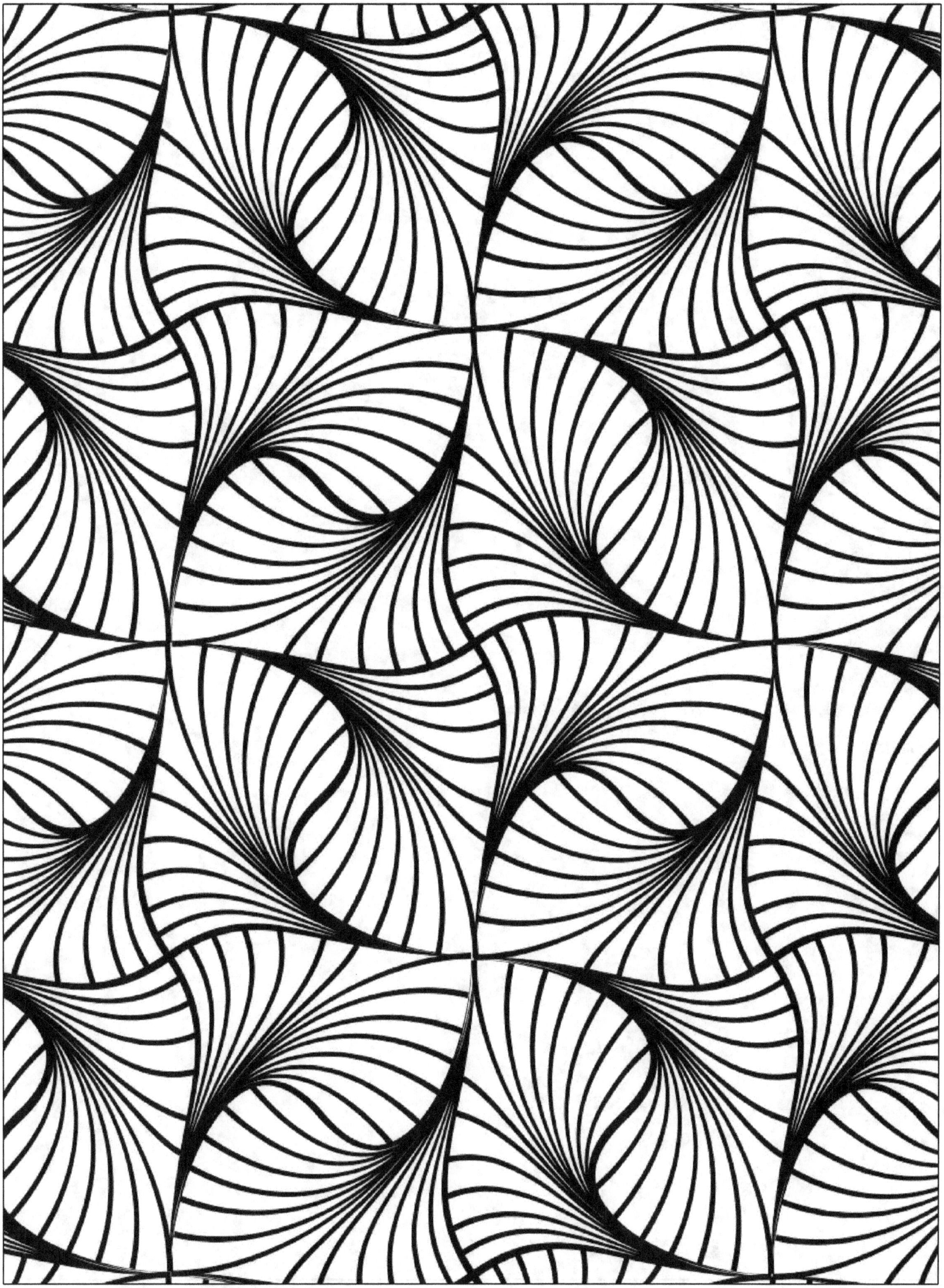

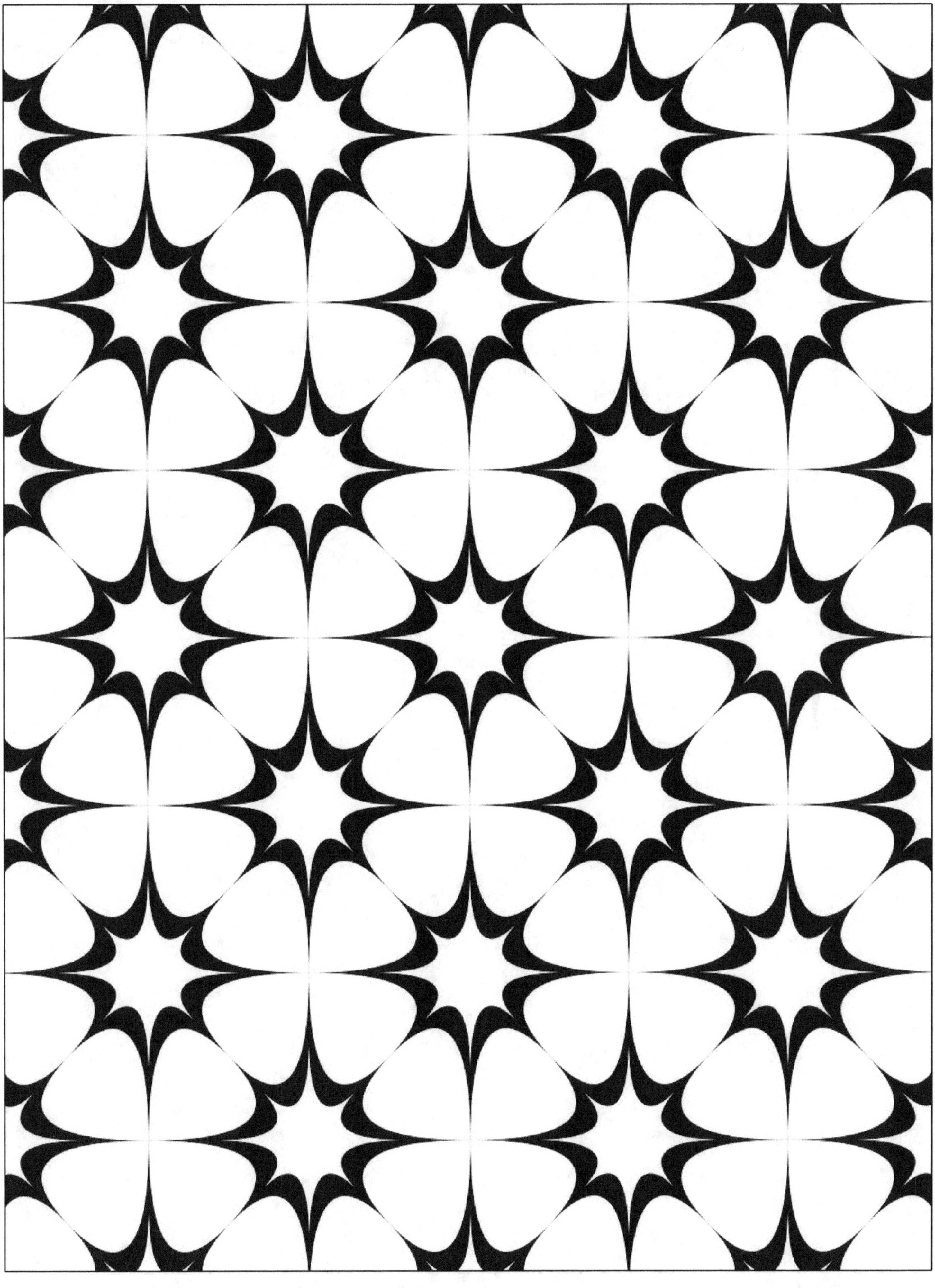

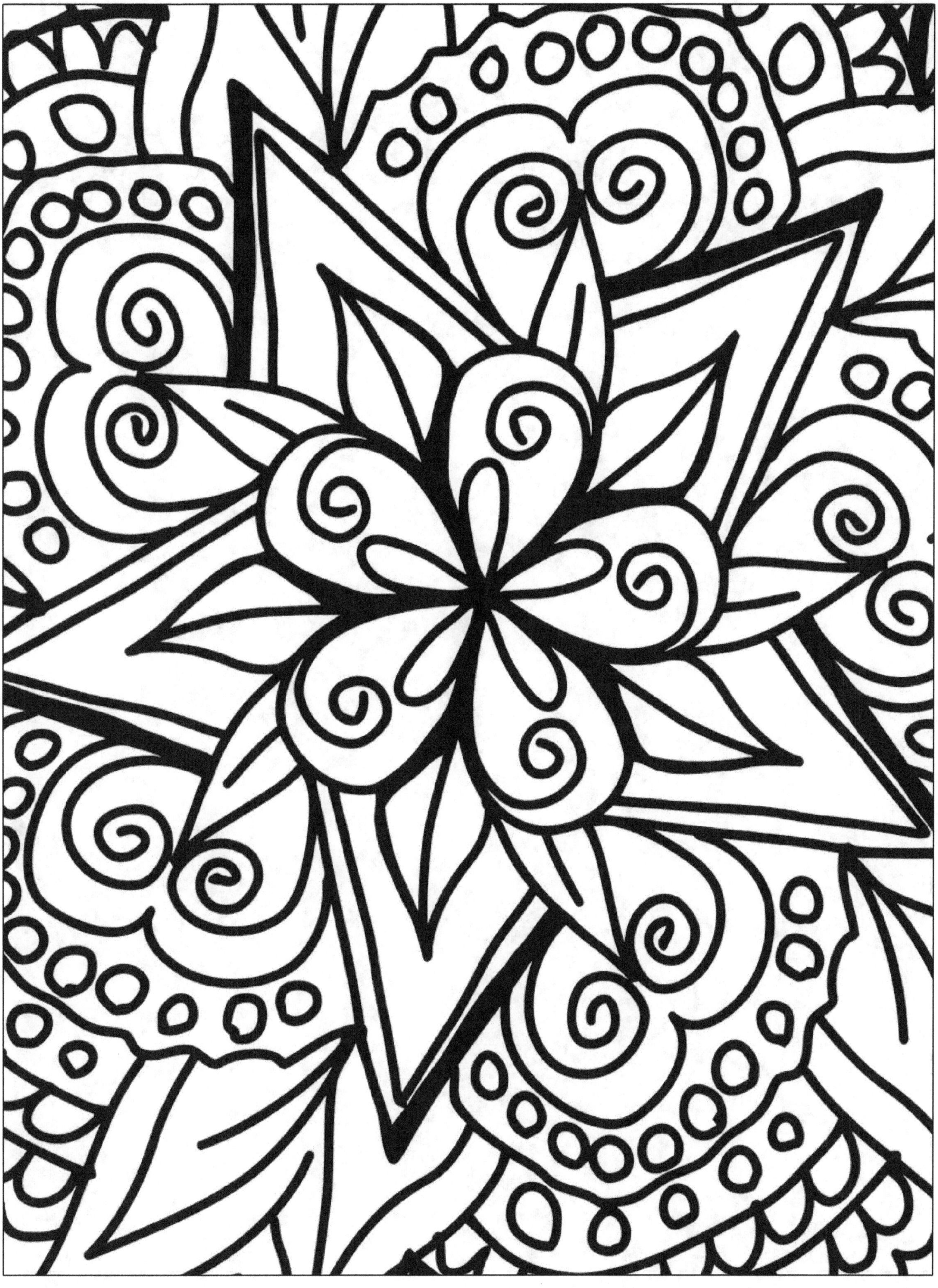

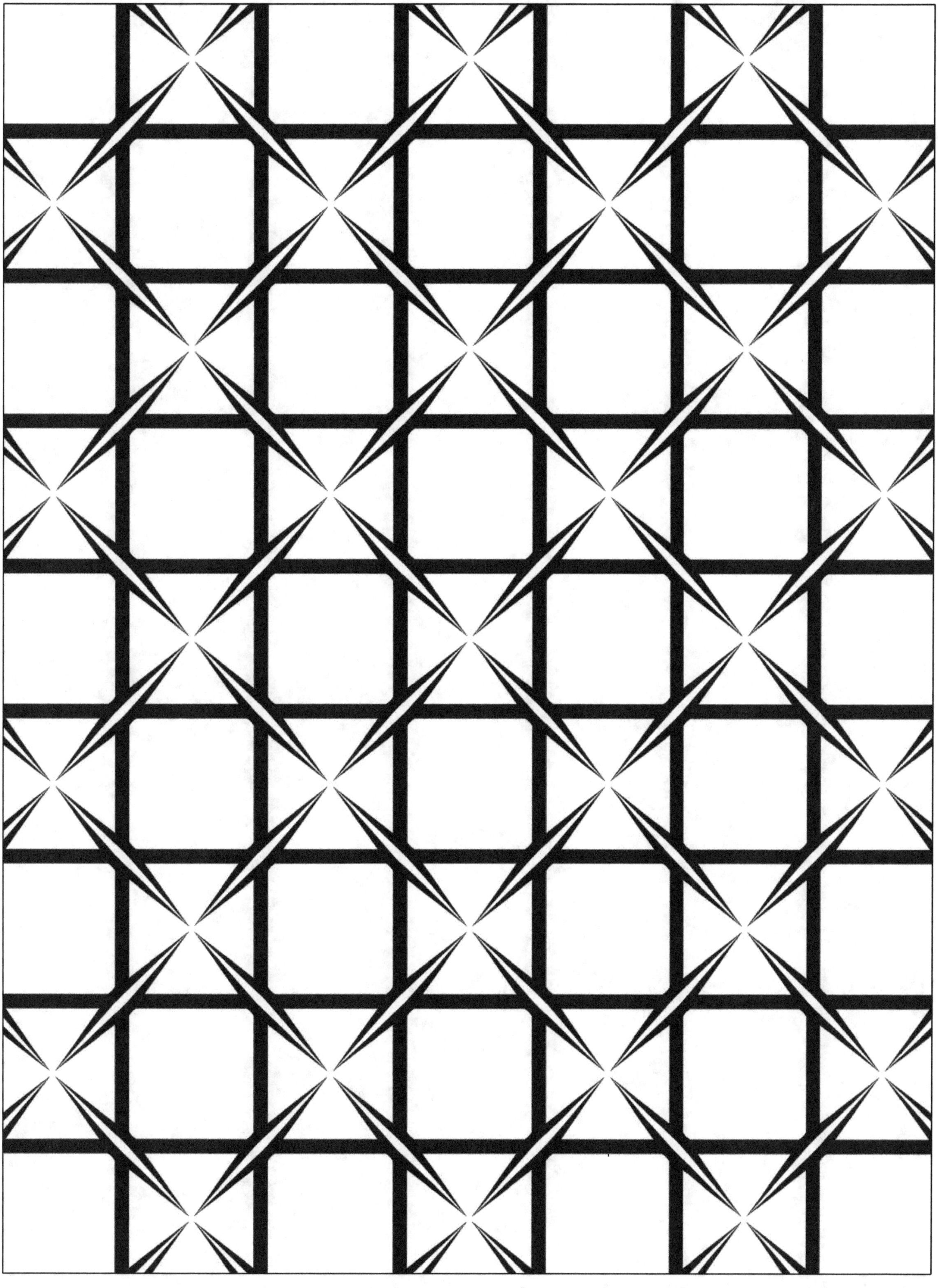

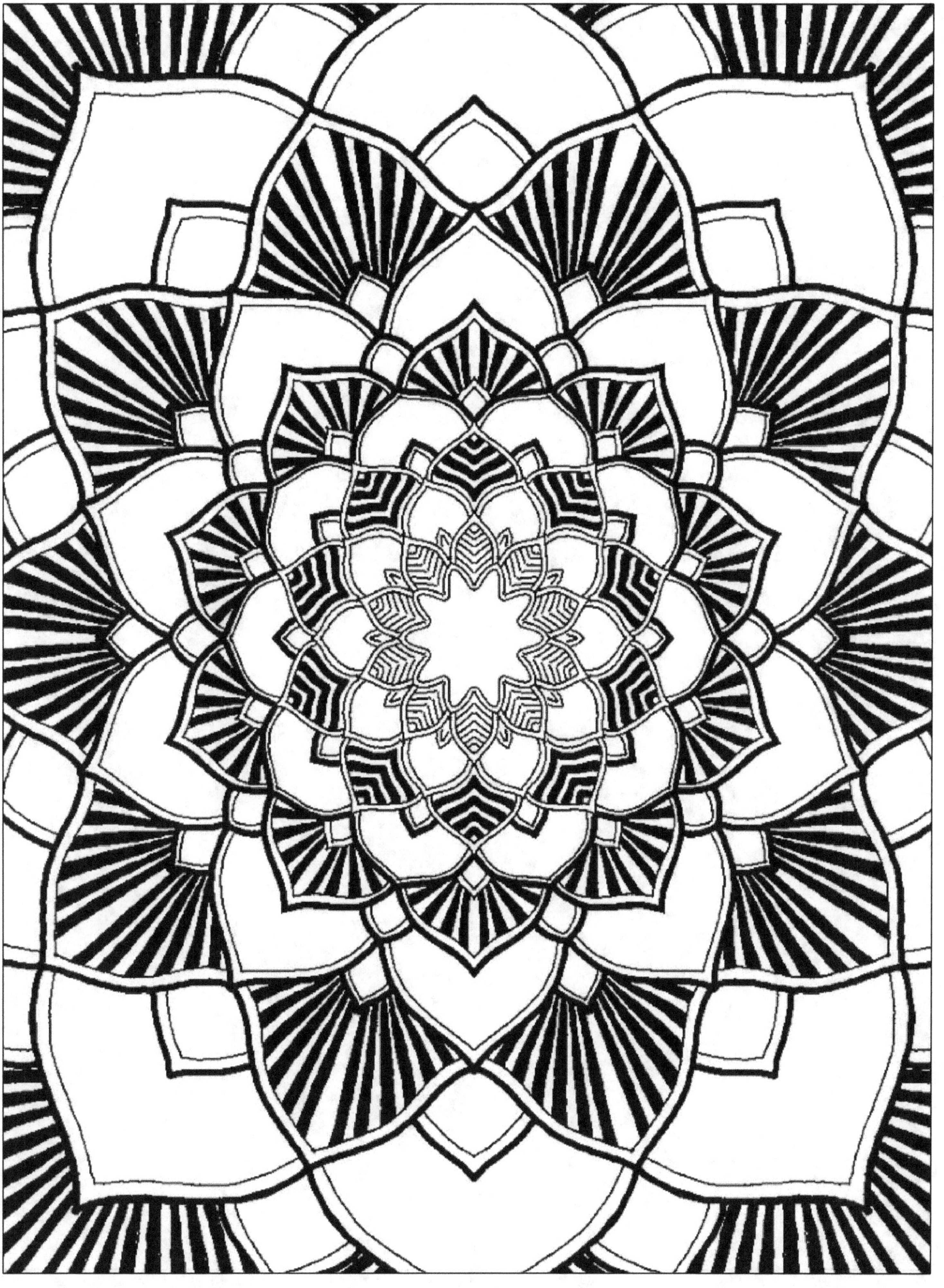

www.ingramcontent.com/pod-product-compliance
Lightning Source LLC
Chambersburg PA
CBHW081525220526
45467CB00010B/3052
* 9 7 9 8 6 9 6 3 8 9 3 9 4 *